T0358450

ROUTLEDGE LIBRARY EDITIONS:
BRITISH IN INDIA

Volume 11

INCOME DISTRIBUTION, GROWTH AND BASIC NEEDS IN INDIA

INCOME DISTRIBUTION, GROWTH AND BASIC NEEDS IN INDIA

R. SINHA, PETER PEARSON, GOPAL
KADEKODI AND MARY GREGORY

Routledge
Taylor & Francis Group

LONDON AND NEW YORK

First published in 1979 by Croom Helm Ltd

This edition first published in 2017
by Routledge
2 Park Square, Milton Park, Abingdon, Oxon OX14 4RN

and by Routledge
711 Third Avenue, New York, NY 10017

Routledge is an imprint of the Taylor & Francis Group, an informa business

British Library Cataloguing in Publication Data
A catalogue record for this book is available from the British Library

ISBN: 978-1-138-22929-7 (Set)
ISBN: 978-1-315-20179-5 (Set) (ebk)
ISBN: 978-1-138-29110-2 (Volume 11) (hbk)
ISBN: 978-1-315-20755-1 (Volume 11) (ebk)

Publisher's Note
The publisher has gone to great lengths to ensure the quality of this reprint but
points out that some imperfections in the original copies may be apparent.

Disclaimer
The publisher has made every effort to trace copyright holders and would welcome
correspondence from those they have been unable to trace.

Income Distribution, Growth and Basic Needs in India

R. Sinha, Peter Pearson, Gopal Kadekodi and Mary Gregory

CROOM HELM LONDON

British Library Cataloguing in Publication Data

Income distribution, growth and basic needs in India.
   1. Income distribution — India — Mathematical
   models   2. India — Economic policy — 1966 —
   Mathematical models
   I. Sinha, Radha
   339.2'0954   HC440.15

ISBN 0-85664-968-6

This book arises from a research project jointly sponsored by the Department of
Political Economy, Glasgow University, the Institute of Economic Growth, Delhi,
and Queen Elizabeth House, Oxford University, and aided by a grant from the
Ministry of Overseas Development, UK. The views expressed are those of the
authors and do not represent the views of the institutions or of the Ministry of
Overseas Development.

Printed in Great Britain by offset lithography by
Billing & Sons Ltd, Guildford, London and Worcester

CONTENTS

TABLES

Figures

ACKNOWLEDGEMENTS

This book is the outcome of a research project sponsored jointly by the Department of Political Economy, Glasgow University, the Institute of Economic Growth, Delhi, and Queen Elizabeth House, Oxford.

The project has been, in a very real sense, a collaborative venture. All four authors have worked on it at various times in both India and Britain, and essential contributions have been made by institutions and individuals in both countries. Much of the early work, including substantial parts of the data assembly and the initial programming, were undertaken over a period of two years at the Institute in Delhi. The final data assembly, the running of the simulations and the writing up subsequently took place in Glasgow.

The successful completion of a large-scale project such as this depends heavily on the contributions of others in addition to the major participants who appear as authors. The list of those who have helped us, on general or specific matters, is long, but our gratitude to each of them is in no way diminished by this.

The idea for the project was originally mooted by Paul Streeten, then of Queen Elizabeth House, and developed in consultation with him and with the participation also of Frances Stewart (Queen Elizabeth House) and John Healey (Ministry of Overseas Development). Professor Tom Wilson of Glasgow University, and Professors A.M. Khusro, P.B. Desai and C.H.H. Rao, successively Directors of the Institute in Delhi, maintained a continuous involvement in the progress of the project and smoothed the path for us, at their respective institutions, in many ways.

A number of specialists gave us invaluable assistance on particular aspects, and their individual contributions are included in our project Report. We are happy to acknowledge the help of (in alphabetical order): Dr Raghav Gaiha, Institute of Economic Growth (manpower); Dr D. B. Gupta, Institute of Economic Growth (small-scale industries); Dr V. G. Jhingran, Director, Central Inland Fisheries Research Institute, Barrackpore (freshwater fisheries); Dr R. N. Lal, National Sample Survey, Delhi (capital formation); Dr G.C. Mathur, Director, National Building Organisation, Delhi (employment aspects of housing construction); Dr G. Pingle, Commonwealth Secretariat, London (cropping pattern and employment, value added in agriculture); Dr M. S. Ramanujam and Mr K. Raghavan, Institute of Applied Manpower Research, Delhi (sectorwise employment); Justice P. Jaganmohan Reddy, retired judge of the Supreme Court of India (constitutional provision for social justice); Mr S. N. Sinha, Member of the Bihar State Planning Board (employment aspects of roads and bridges); and Mr M. R. Saluja, Indian Statistical Institute, Delhi (construction of input-output table).

Others whose expert advice and assistance we are happy to acknowledge are: Professor R. Diwan, Rensselaer Polytechnic Institute, Troy, USA (conceptualisation and measurement of unemployment); Dr D. N. Dwivedi, Ramjas College, Delhi (taxation); Mr S. M. Luthra, Delhi University Computing Centre (programming of the simulation model); Dr G. P. Mishra, then at Ranchi University and now at the Institute for Social and Economic Change, Bangalore (value added in agriculture); Mr M. R. Rao, Planning Commission Computing Department (programming advice); and Dr P. Venkatramaiah, Gokhale Institute of Politics and Economics, Poona (input-output advice).

We are thankful to Dr S. R. Bowlby (Reading University) for her assistance given in programming, and Messrs G. O'Donnell and M. Partridge (Glasgow University) for their assistance in clarification of methodological issues, and to Dr M. G. Mueller (Glasgow University) for continual advice and support on data sources and analytical materials on income distribution, both national and international. The presence of Dr D. B. Gupta (who was on the Project's Technical Advisory Committee in the Institute of Economic Growth, Delhi) at the University of Hull, England, at the time of finalising the draft Report proved to be of great value. We are also thankful to Dr G. Pingle (Commonwealth Secretariat, London) for reading the draft of the Report and making valuable suggestions. Among the many others to whom we owe a deep sense of gratitude for helping in various ways, mention should be made of Justice P. Jaganmohan Reddy, Dr J. S. Sarma, Secretary of the National Commission on Agriculture, New Delhi, Dr M. T. R. Sarma of the National Council of Applied Economic Research, New Delhi, Dr Manmohan Singh, Secretary to the Finance Ministry, Mr R. J. Perkins (FAO), Dr F. Paukert (ILO) and Dr K. Krishnamurty (IMF). Helpful comments on the project Report were received from Dr Solon L. Barraclough (Director, UNRISD, Geneva), Dr Wouter van Ginneken (ILO), Professor Martin Bronfenbrenner and Dr Richard Weisskoff.

We are thankful to Mr K. K. Agrawal, Miss A. K. Bharadwaj, Mr P. Bhowmik, Mr P. Ghosh, Mr P. Manchanda, Mr K. C. Rao and Miss B. Saraswati for their technical assistance at Delhi in the collation of data.

We are also grateful to the staff responsible for computing facilities in the Adam Smith Building, for their unfailing help over the past few years and to Mr S. K. Gupta in Delhi, Mrs F. Dick, Ms J. Stillie, Miss E. O'Donnell, Mrs M. Feasby and Miss J. Weir in Glasgow, for secretarial help and reproduction of the Report and the working papers.

We are extremely grateful to Miss M. Travis, Librarian, Indian High Commission Library, London, for meeting often excessive demands for research materials.

Last, but not least, we wish to acknowledge our debt to the Ministry of Overseas Development for financing the research, and in particular Mr R. S. Porter, Director General of Economic Planning, for his help and encouragement in the initial stages.

It goes without saying that none of the institutions or individuals mentioned above is in any way responsible for any of the views expressed or any errors or omissions made. These remain the responsibility of the authors.

Radha Sinha

Project Director

ABBREVIATIONS

AIR	All India Radio
AIRDIS	All India Rural Debt and Investment Survey
ASI	Annual Survey of Industries
CIFRI	Central Inland Fisheries Research Institute
CMI	Census of Manufacturing Industries
CPWD	Central Public Works Department
CRRI	Central Road Research Institute
CSO	Central Statistical Organisation
DGCI	Directorate General of Commercial Intelligence
DGET	Directorate General of Employment and Training
DGSD	Directorate General of Supplies and Disposal
DGTD	Directorate General of Technical Development
DPAP	Drought Prone Areas Programme
EA	Office of the Economic Adviser
EMI	Employment Market Information
EMIP	Employment Market Information Programme
FAO	UN Food and Agriculture Organisation
FMS	Farm Management Surveys
IARS	The Institute of Agricultural Research Statistics
ICAR	Indian Council of Agricultural Research
ICMR	Indian Council of Medical Research
ILCAME	Indian Livestock Census on Agricultural Machinery and Equipment
ISI	Indian Statistical Institute
LB	Labour Bureau
MFAL	Marginal Farmers'and Agricultural Labourers' Programmes
MSPSI	Monthly Statistics of Production of Selected Industries
NBO	National Buildings Organisation
NCA	National Commission on Agriculture
NCAER	National Council of Applied Economic Research
NCO	National Classification of Occupations
NSS	National Sample Survey
RBI	Reserve Bank of India
RGO	Office of the Registrar General of Census of India

SFDA	Small Farmer Development Agency
SSMI	Sample Survey of Manufacturing Industries
USAID	United States Agency for International Development
WHO	UN World Health Organisation

INTRODUCTION

Interest in income distribution, in the forces which shape it and its implications for the welfare of the community, has waxed and waned over many years. Similarly, the status of groups which are disadvantaged and in poverty has received periodic attention, sometimes in the enunciation of political principles or policies and sometimes as a subject for research. Recently, these various strands have been woven together in the strategy of 'basic needs'. Proponents of this strategy want a commitment, at national and international levels, to securing the provision of at least the minimum means of livelihood for everyone, through redistribution and growth.

Any approach aimed at providing for basic needs must face one of its most searching tests in India, where the problem of poverty is immense both in depth and extent. Even on an austere definition, possibly 200 million people, roughly one-third of the Indian population, exist below the poverty line. Moreover, the poor of India represent almost two-thirds of those estimated to be below the poverty line in the continents of Asia, Africa and Latin America. No provision for basic needs can be considered to be a successful international development programme if it is not also achieved in India.

Undoubtedly, a major reason for the emergence of the basic needs strategy may be found in the humanitarian motive which seeks to eliminate or at least reduce the deprivation of that large section of world population which does not seem to have gained significantly from the economic development of recent decades. Many national growth rates, particularly in poorer countries, have been respectable, even impressive, by any standards; nevertheless, many large groups, often of the poorest people, are no better off and may even be worse off than before the 'drive to development' began.

The motives which prompt concern with the reduction of poverty and with distributional issues are not, however, confined purely to the humanitarian. For those associated with both the politics and the economics of development, nationally and internationally, the matter has been forced to the fore by the apparently impressive progress made by the other Asian giant, the People's Republic of China, against semi-starvation and inadequate employment opportunities. Furthermore, also at the political level, some political and intellectual leaders in the

Third World harbour the suspicion that the basic needs strategy is being emphasised by the richer countries essentially in order to divert attention from Third World demands for the restructuring of the world economy, of the type postulated in the 'New International Economic Order'.

Whatever the underlying motives, the current prominence of the basic needs strategy in the international arena adds urgency to the exploration of the inter-relations between poverty, income distribution and employment. Our study aims to contribute to this exploration, both in the elaboration of a methodological approach and through its application to India as one of the countries in which poverty poses the greatest challenge.

On the methodological side, we present a model which incorporates the distribution of personal incomes into the income-expenditure-output framework familiarly adopted in macro-economic analysis. The key feature of this model lies in the generation of the distribution of incomes, by income class and in rural and urban areas separately, through the structure of earnings created in each industry. In addition, the distribution of incomes itself affects the level and pattern of expenditure through the differing consumption behaviour of the various groups. The distribution of incomes is thus integrated into the model through both its origins in production and its impact on expenditure.

Using this framework, we are able to simulate the implications for the distribution of incomes, as well as for production and employment, of a wide variety of changes in output, expenditure or incomes. Moreover, since the identification of groups below the poverty line was a consideration influencing the delineation of the socio-economic classes in the model, we are able in particular to trace the implications of these changes for the position of the poor. The model is used to simulate the effects of a number of possible developments and policies. These include: income transfers from rich to poor; growth strategies based on alternative groups of sectors, such as light or heavy industry; hypothetical policies of growth-with-redistribution; and a land redistribution.

Models which are comparable in concept with ours have been proposed for only a very few countries; and even where this framework has been suggested, estimation has not always been carried out. We believe that this study represents the first attempt to apply a model of this structure to the analysis of income distribution and basic needs in India. Not unexpectedly, the problems of data availability, quality and compatibility have been formidable. This is especially true of the area in which we break most new ground, the estimation of the distribution of personal incomes from the 77 individual producing sectors. While we would not wish to claim that all the numerical estimates are of perfect accuracy, or even that our methodology is complete or unflawed, the complexity and often initially surprising nature of the pattern of income flows revealed strongly suggests that an adequate treatment of distributional issues can be achieved only through the explicit linking of the distribution of incomes with both production and expenditure. Given the importance and urgency of the problem of poverty, we hope that doubts about the conceptual adequacy or the numerical accuracy of the results presented here will serve as a stimulus to further work.

Our study begins with a brief historical perspective on attitudes towards distributional questions and the provision for basic needs in modern political thought in India. We then consider in more detail the concept of basic needs and the definition of the poverty line, with particular emphasis on the current position of the poor in India. In Chapter 2 we describe the structure of the model, and consider the issues involved in the specification of its constituent parts. Chapter 3 reports our major data innovation, the construction of a matrix of coefficients for the distribution of personal incomes, by income class and between rural and urban areas, individually for each of the 77 sectors of our industrial classification.

The following three chapters describe the main empirical and conceptual findings of our research, in the form of results from simulations through the model of various potential developments or policies. Chapter 4 presents the full structure of income flows as model simulations reveal them. The implications of income transfers from rich to poor are then traced, with particular attention paid to the size of the transfers necessary to double the incomes of the poor; this is a first, although limited, attempt to ensure a provision for basic needs. The chapter concludes with a tentative exploration of the consequences of structural change, in the form of land redistribution as an alternative to income redistribution.

Since access to employment opportunities is itself of fundamental importance to the poor, Chapter 5 is devoted to the potential for employment creation. We begin by reporting our estimates of the employment intensity of individual sectors and also of the consumption baskets of the various income classes. The chapter concludes with an assessment of the potential for employment creation through changes in either the distribution of incomes or the pattern of output.

In Chapter 6 we examine the implications of growth for the distribution of incomes and for the position of the poor. We consider a variety of possible growth strategies based on alternative leading sectors. Further simulations involve hypothetical policies of growth-with-redistribution, in the form of growth strategies in which the increase in income is channelled to target income groups. The chapter concludes with an examination of the consequences of a 50 per cent growth in gross domestic product for the level and distribution of personal incomes.

The concluding chapter reviews our findings, first in a methodological context, through an assessment of the strengths and limitations of the model structure, and finally in the context of policies currently adopted and current debates on policy issues in India.

1 A PERSPECTIVE ON INCOME DISTRIBUTION AND BASIC NEEDS

The basic needs strategy, in its current broad formulation, is conceived as an attack on deprivation in its two major facets: physical deprivation due to inadequate means of subsistence, and the associated deprivation of basic human rights. The essential concepts involved are defined by the International Labour Office (ILO):[1]

> First, they include certain minimum requirements of a family for private consumption: adequate food, shelter and clothing are obviously included, as would be certain household equipment and furniture.
> Second, they include essential services provided by and for the community at large, such as safe drinking water, sanitation, public transport, and health and educational facilities.

And more fundamentally:

> A basic-needs oriented policy implies the participation of the people in making the decisions which affect them. Participation interacts with the two main elements of a basic-needs strategy. For example, education and good health will facilitate participation, and participation in turn will strengthen the claim for the material basic needs.
> The satisfaction of an absolute level of basic needs as so defined should be placed within a broader framework — namely the fulfilment of basic human rights, which are not only ends in themselves but also contribute to the attainment of other goals. (ILO, 1976, p. 32)

While this mode of formulation and the international context are contemporary developments, the political and intellectual leaders of modern India have, from the earliest days, held clearly articulated views and beliefs about the guaranteeing of both physical needs and human rights.

As Bronfenbrenner (1971, p. 3) points out at the beginning of his seminal study of the theory of income distribution, 'The classical-

economist and classical-Socialist concern with distribution and redistri-
bution has become especially marked in India.' As early as 1937 the
National Planning Committee appointed by the All-India Congress
Committee (AICC) had stressed that:

> The ideal of the Congress is the establishment of a free and demo-
> cratic State in India. Such a full democratic State involves an egali-
> tarian society, in which equal opportunities are provided for every
> member for self-expression and self-fulfilment, and *an adequate
> minimum of a civilised standard of life* [our italics] is assured to
> each member so as to make the attainment of this equal oppor-
> tunity a reality. (Quoted in Madan, 1966, p. 302)

Again, in its election manifesto of 1945 the AICC gave a pledge much
on the same lines:

> Industry and agriculture, the social services and public utilities must
> be encouraged, modernised and rapidly extended in order to add to
> the wealth of the country and give it the capacity for self-growth
> without dependence on others. But all this must be done with the
> primary object of benefitting the masses of our people and raising
> their economic, cultural and spiritual levels, removing unemploy-
> ment and adding to the dignity of the individual. (p. 304)

Thus the objective and main elements of the 'basic needs' strategy, in
conjunction with self-sustained growth of the economy, had already
been fully recognised and adopted as the principal aims of economic
planning in India even before Independence.

The commitment to them on Independence was clearly affirmed in
the Constituent Assembly in the course of the constitutional debate. In
the words of Nehru, one of the chief architects of modern India and the
main inspiration behind Indian planning, 'The first task of this
Assembly . . . is to free India through a new constitution, to feed the
starving people, and to clothe the naked masses, and to give every
Indian the fullest opportunity to develop himself according to his
capacity.'[2]

The Indian leadership always viewed its task in terms of three revo-
lutions: political, social and economic. The political revolution ended
with Independence. Social revolution meant the elimination of medieval-
ism based on birth, religion, custom and community, and the recon-
struction of the social structure on modern foundations of law,

individual merit, and secular education. The economic revolution was to consist of the 'transition from primitive rural economy to scientific and planned agriculture and industry'.[3] As Radhakrishnan, the well-known philosopher, among many others, underlined, a 'socio-economic revolution' in India has not only to attain 'the real satisfaction of the fundamental needs of the common man' but also to go much deeper and bring about a fundamental restructuring of Indian society (Austin, 1966, p. 27). And the Indian leaders were also conscious that time was limited 'because the Indian masses cannot and will not wait for a long time to obtain the satisfaction of their minimum needs' (p. 27).

While there was widespread agreement among Indian leaders on these social and economic objectives, views differed on how they were to be achieved. Nehru's commitment to modernisation and centralised planning is well known.[4] Under the influence of Mahatma Gandhi (henceforth, Mahatma) the Congress Party and the Constituent Assembly pressed for the recognition of self-sufficient, self-governing villages as the primary units of social reorganisation. Mahatma had always preached

> the growth of cities to be an evil thing, unfortunate for mankind and the world . . . and certainly unfortunate for India . . . The British have exploited India through its cities. The latter have exploited the villages. The blood of the villages is the cement with which the edifice of the cities is built. I want the blood that is today inflating the arteries of the cities to run once again in the blood vessels of the villages.[5]

Although the idea of a highly decentralised Gandhian model was given up under the influence of the 'modernisers' and the 'unifiers' of Nehru's persuasion, a number of essential features of Gandhian ideology were nevertheless incorporated in the Constitution under the provisions concerning fundamental rights and the Directive Principles of State Policy.[6]

With a view to giving equality real meaning it was provided that the state should not discriminate against any citizen on the grounds of religion, race, caste or sex. This provision was expressly extended to cover access to shops, hotels, restaurants, etc., and to the use of wells, tanks and roads maintained out of public funds (Panikkar, 1963, p. 158). Equality of opportunity in matters of public employment was guaranteed to women also. Untouchability was formally abolished and its practice made an offence (p. 159). Special provisions were made in

terms of reservations of seats in the legislatures, jobs and educational
institutions, for the Scheduled Castes (untouchables or *harijans*) and
Scheduled Tribes.

The Directive Principles of State, though not justiciable, but to be
considered 'fundamental in the governance of the country', emphati-
cally laid down that the 'State shall strive to promote the welfare of the
people by securing and protecting as effectively as it may a social order
in which justice, social, economic and political, shall inform all the
institutions of national life' (Austin, p. 52). The state was exhorted:

> to ensure that citizens have an adequate means of livelihood, that
> the operation of the economic system and the ownership and
> control of the material resources of the country subserve the
> common good, that the health of the workers, including children,
> is not abused and that special consideration is given to pregnant
> women. (p. 52)

Moreover, the Principles stress the importance of providing for nutrition, education and leisure, as well as the contribution to be made by
improving the techniques of production.

Thus it is clear that the fundamental elements now making up the
basic needs strategy, in its domestic aspects, have not only been current
in Indian political thought for more than a generation but are formally
embedded in the Indian Constitution. Acceptance of the objectives,
clearly posited, has never been a major problem. Nor, except perhaps in
the very earliest years, has the leadership underestimated the immensity
of the task involved.[7] In spite of this, however, a problem of enormous
magnitude remains.

The Poverty Line

The two themes of the basic needs strategy, the ensuring of physical
subsistence and of basic human rights, are obviously interdependent.
But since the central focus of this study is the distribution of income
our analysis will concentrate on the aspect of the requirements for
physical subsistence. In order to implement a strategy of basic needs,
even confined to this more limited objective, a necessary prerequisite
is the definition of the poverty line and the identification of the target
groups.

Various estimates have been made of the poverty line in India and of
the proportion of the population subsisting below it. These studies
follow a common methodology. First, the nutritionally 'minimum'

balanced diet for an 'average' person is identified and costed; the figure so obtained is then blown up by a ratio of food to total expenditure in order to account for necessary minimum expenditure on non-food items.

One of the earliest studies of this kind is by a study group of the Planning Commission of India; it estimated Rs 20 per month at 1960-1 prices as the bare minimum level of living, with no allowance for any expenditure on health and education. Several other estimates broadly confirm this. In his various studies Bardhan typically uses Rs 15 for rural and Rs 18 for urban areas (Bardhan, 1974, p. 120), while Dandekar and Rath (1971) suggest the same figure for rural but the higher figure of Rs 22.5 for urban areas (all at 1960-1 prices).[8] On the basis of these estimates Bardhan has suggested that in 1968-9 as many as 54 per cent of the rural population were below the poverty line, along with 41 per cent of the urban population. Dandekar and Rath, on the other hand, almost exactly reverse these rural/urban proportions, finding the relatively greater incidence of poverty to be in the urban areas, a view broadly shared by the United Nations Economic Commission for Asia and the Far East (UNECAFE, 1972, p. 51). More recently an official estimate based on the National Sample Survey (NSS) suggests that in 1973-4 around 46 per cent of the total population were below the poverty line, while Planning Commission figures for 1977-8 suggest 48 per cent of the rural population and 41 per cent of the urban population.[9] While these various studies, with their differing reference dates, show a broad measure of agreement, other and much more diverse estimates have also been made. Bhatty, for example, using income distribution data from the National Council of Applied Economic Research (NCAER) for 1967-8 and different poverty levels ranging between Rs 15 and Rs 35 finds up to 70 per cent of the rural population below the poverty line (Bhatty, 1974, p. 300).

Apart from the different reference years, the variation in these estimates has several sources. The minimum necessary calorie intake is variously defined, usually between 2,100 and 2,400 per day. The composition of the diet incorporating the minimum nutritional requirements similarly varies, and in a country of the geographic size and ethnic complexity of India any single diet can be only an approximation The prices used in costing the diet and the expenditure distribution into which the poverty line is projected are similarly liable to variation. For these various reasons no single figure can be adopted with certainty and precision.

A more fundamental criticism of the methodology comes, however,

from Sukhatme (1977). He argues that the recommended nutritional
requirement (of say 2,400 or 2,200 calories) is a recommended average
and not a minimum. This in itself suggests that, in a population which
is normally distributed with respect to height, weight, activity rate, etc.,
half the people will have a calorie requirement below this recommended
average. It is only by comparing the distribution of requirements
against the distribution of intake that one can find the actual number
of undernourished persons. He stresses:

> Even a priori, the use of average calorie requirement as the criterion
> for classifying a person as undernourished cannot be justified, for to
> consider that anyone eating below the average need is undernouri-
> shed is equivalent to considering that anyone eating above the
> average need is overnourished. Such a classification would amount
> to considering that the average requirement is both a desirable
> minimum and optimum to aim at at the same time. To do so is to
> deny the existence of inter individual variation altogether . . . There
> must be a normal range of intake within which an individual is able
> to maintain his health, activity and energy balance over extended
> periods, without implying that he is undernourished whenever his
> intake falls below his average need and vice versa. (pp. 4-5)

On Sukhatme's adjustment of the distribution of requirements against
the distribution of intake, the estimated population below the poverty
line is reduced to 25 per cent in the urban and 15 per cent in the rural
areas (p. 16), a very substantial reduction relative to the estimates
quoted above.[10]

   An alternative methodology, which has elements in common with
that of Sukhatme, has been developed by FAO and used in their estimates of the undernourished population in India (United Nations FAO,
1977, p. 127). Starting from the concept of Basal Metabolic Rate
(BMR), the energy cost of human body maintenance, without any
allowance for activities, the FAO set a critical minimum limit at 1.2
BMR. Those persons with a food intake below this critical limit are in
all probability suffering from some form of energy deprivation (United
Nations FAO/WHO, 1973, p. 36). On this basis any person getting less
than 1,486 calories would fall in this category. The proportion of such
people in 1972-4 was estimated to be about 30 per cent of the total
population or around 175 million (p. 127).

   A further possible source of inaccuracy in the conventional methodology for estimating the poverty line relates to the practice of blowing

up the estimated cost of the necessary diet by a fixed ratio between food and non-food expenditure as obtained from consumption surveys. This presupposes that the recorded levels of food and non-food expenditure fall short of their basic minimum standards in the same proportions. The direction of the bias because of this, however, cannot be easily established; the basic minimum food expenditure may be even harder to reduce than the minimum on other items, but on the other hand it is possible that payments such as rent, as compulsory demands on the household, are maintained at the expense of food.

Estimates of the proportion of the population in poverty are typically based on household consumption surveys and may fail to capture intrafamily inequities. Even families above, perhaps significantly above, the poverty line may include members who are seriously undernourished. Women and children most often come into this category. A survey conducted by the National Institute of Nutrition found that the average daily intake of pregnant and lactating women was as low as 1,400 calories, against the average Indian requirement of 2,200 calories (National Institute of Nutrition, 1971, Table XVI). In another survey it was found that, on average, only 58 per cent of the calorie needs of pregnant and lactating mothers between the ages of 15 and 19 were being met (USAID, 1975, vol. 1, Tables 11-12). This study also indicated that for weaned children in the 7-18 months' age group only 65 per cent of the calorie needs were met; in the case of non-weaned children the figure was as low as 52 per cent (p. 92).

No one who has been involved in studying these problems would claim that the poverty line is, or can be, a precise measuring rod. Even if one accepts the very lowest of the available estimates, Sukhatme's of 15 to 25 per cent of the population below the poverty line − or even FAO's estimate of 30 per cent − the number of people involved would still range between 110 and 175 million. The immensity of the human problem which this implies cannot be dismissed with numerical quibbling.

In spite of its usefulness in indicating the general magnitude of the problem of poverty, the poverty line, like any other composite index, monetary or non-monetary, cannot give much guidance in identifying the main contributory factors and devising appropriate solutions. It is important, therefore, that such composite indices are supplemented, as far as data availability permits, by a close look at other, and more disaggregated, main indicators.

Identifying the Target Groups

The target groups have long been recognised in India, at least in very broad and general terms. The Indian Constituent Assembly (1947) enumerated what it regarded as the most vulnerable groups in Indian society, and made the first of various specific legal provisions for the improvement of their economic, social and educational status. Various court decisions since the inauguration of the new Constitution have confirmed the interpretation of backwardness not only in terms of castes and tribes but also of socio-economic and educational status.

It has been generally recognised that the target groups of the poor and underprivileged comprise mainly landless agricultural labourers, tenant farmers and small peasant proprietors in the rural areas, and the unemployed and the underemployed in the urban areas. This categorisation will probably apply irrespective of caste status. Nevertheless, it is true that the proportion of landless labourers and tenants, etc. is much higher among the so-called 'backward classes' than in their 'high caste' counterparts; it does not necessarily mean that the latter are always economically better off than the former.[11] It is quite possible that a high caste primary school teacher in a rural area is economically worse off than a tenant farmer or, in some cases, 'low caste' landless labourer with regular employment. Similarly, high caste households of a school teacher or clerk in an urban area may have a considerably lower income and nutritional status than the households of domestic servants.

However, by and large, it can be suggested that the people who fall in the lowest income groups in the rural areas are normally the landless labourers, the unemployed, the underemployed and smallholders (either owners or tenants). The urban unemployed and underemployed, and the new migrants, also fall in this group (Sinha, 1976, p. 12). Landless labourers suffer most, particularly because the employment open to them is largely seasonal. Smallholders – both owner-operators and tenants – are also poorly placed, particularly those who have to supplement their income by working as wage labour on others' farms. A substantial number of landless labourers and smallholders are forced by circumstances – lack of jobs, loss of land as a result of non-payment of debts or simply eviction by landlords[12] – to migrate to towns and cities in search of jobs, thereby exacerbating the problems of urban unemployment and slum conditions of living.

In the present study, because of the structure of our model and lack of data to identify groups more closely, we define classes on the basis of income. For both rural and urban areas the total population is divided into bottom, middle and top income groups, each consisting of approximately one-third of the total population. Though our classification is income based, each of our classes approximates to a particular socio-economic category. The bottom group in rural areas consists largely of landless labourers, and smallholders, tenants as well as owner-operators. The middle group consists for the most part of medium farmers, along with small-scale operators in handicrafts, trades, etc. Large farmers, the rural population engaged in large-scale urban industry, mining and construction, and people engaged in trade and money lending will constitute the top income category. Similarly, in the urban areas the unemployed and the underemployed in what is known as the 'informal sector' largely fall in the bottom groups; most industrial workers come into the middle income group, while the top group comprises professionals, upper civil servants and prosperous business people.

Average Consumption and Basic Needs

Before concentrating attention specifically on the position of the poorer groups, a sobering perspective can be gained on the immensity of the problem of poverty in India as a whole by first considering average consumption levels across the entire population. The geographical, cultural, ethnic and other diversities of India, in addition to its sheer size, inevitably imply a wide degree of variation around the average. In this macro-study we incorporate only one, but arguably nationally the most significant, source of diversity, the rural-urban dimension. Average consumption levels will be assessed for these two populations separately and their consumption patterns compared.

The average level of rural *per capita* consumption is just under three-quarters the average urban level (Table 1.1, page 32). Consumption of food grains is somewhat higher in the rural than in the urban areas, while consumption expenditure on fruits and vegetables, livestock products, edible oils and miscellaneous foods is somewhat lower.[13] Total food expenditure in rural areas is only about 87 per cent of urban expenditure. On the whole, in rural areas food expenditure constitutes roughly three-quarters of the total consumers' expenditure while in urban areas it is only around 62 per cent. Urban food consumption seems to be rather more diversified in terms of quality foods.

The disadvantage of the rural areas in food consumption is, however, probably largely deceptive, owing to lower prices and to some under-recording in rural areas. Consumption of most of the major items in rural areas is based on imputed values, particularly of domestically produced goods or wages received in kind; in urban areas the majority of these involve cash transactions. On the assumption that urban prices in general are 8 per cent higher than rural prices (Kadekodi, 1978, Table 5n), rural consumption becomes 78 per cent of the average urban level. Other estimates, however, suggest a significantly higher price discrepancy, as great as 15 per cent, raising rural consumption to around 83 per cent of the urban level (Chatterjee and Bhattacharya, 1974, p. 195). Moreover, it is likely that recorded consumption omits a proportion of home-grown fruits and vegetables, or those collected from roadside trees and forests; these omissions are likely to be significantly more important in the case of rural households. Similarly, it is likely that domestically produced milk, and meat from animals slaughtered domestically, as well as individual trapping of birds, animals and fish, are underestimated. With allowance for these sources of discrepancy and for the probably rather greater nutritional content of rural consumption, it is quite possible that overall food consumption standards are not very different between rural and urban areas, in spite of the lower rural levels of consumption expenditure.

Table 1.1: Level and Pattern of Consumption in Rural and Urban Areas, 1967-8 (In Rs *per capita*)[*]

Item	Rural Consumption		Urban Consumption		Rural/ urban ratio
Foodgrains	174.6	(36.0)	141.2	(21.1)	1.24
Fruits and vegetables	46.3	(9.6)	77.8	(11.6)	0.60
Livestock products, fish and eggs	50.5	(10.4)	87.5	(13.1)	0.58
Sugar and gur	24.4	(5.0)	16.7	(2.5)	1.46
Vanspati and other vegetable oils	18.3	(3.8)	35.9	(5.4)	0.51
Miscellaneous foods including tea, coffee and tobacco	43.3	(8.9)	51.1	(7.7)	0.85
Total food	357.4	(73.7)	410.2	(61.5)	0.87
Textiles including footwear and leather products	39.1	(8.1)	53.1	(8.0)	0.74
Other manufactures	16.7	(3.4)	42.2	(6.3)	0.40
Total manufactures	55.8	(11.5)	95.3	(14.3)	0.59
Fuel and light (a)	2.8	(0.6)	7.8	(1.2)	0.36
Education (b)	3.8	(0.8)	15.4	(2.3)	0.25
Medical (c)	8.5	(1.8)	17.9	(2.7)	0.47
Services (d)	56.5	(11.7)	120.6	(18.1)	0.47
Total other items	71.6	(14.8)	161.7	(24.2)	0.44
Total consumption	484.8	(100)	667.2	(100)	0.73

[*]Figures within parentheses represent percentages.
a. Includes forestry, coal, coal and petroleum products, and electricity.
b. Includes paper products, printing and education.
c. Includes cosmetic and medicine and medical expenses.
d. Includes railway and other transport, entertainment, domestic and other services, and house rent.
Source: own estimates, based on sectoral consumption from input-output table, with rural and urban proportions from NSS and NCAER.

In non-food expenditure, however, the difference between rural and urban standards is significant. Rural expenditure on cloth and footwear is about three-quarters of urban consumption, while in the case of other manufactures, fuel and light,[14] education, medical and services, rural *per capita* consumption is much less than half of the urban level.[15]

It is highly instructive to compare these average consumption levels with basic needs. In Table 1.2 we show actual *per capita* annual expenditure, on food and in total, for both rural and urban areas, against a set of our own estimates for basic needs. These are based on the recommendations by the Indian Council for Medical Research (ICMR) for a balanced diet for India. They are devised for a vegetarian diet (including some milk) for people in sedentary activities.[16] We feel these estimates are on the high side because the ICMR recommendations (Gopalan and Narasingarao, 1971) are very liberal in terms of livestock products, fish and eggs, and also with regard to calories where they recommend 2,400 against FAO's 2,250. Achieving such diets may be an appropriate long-term aim, but is beyond feasibility in the short run.

It is evident from Table 1.2 that on average both the rural and urban consumption levels fall short of their respective basic minimum levels. The shortfall in rural areas is about 10 per cent for food, and 8 per cent for total consumption expenditure; the corresponding figures for urban areas are 9 per cent and 5 per cent. Thus even on the average in both areas minimum needs are not met. Moreover, it appears that in terms of the relationship between total expenditure and the estimated basic minimum, the rural areas are somewhat more impoverished than the urban.

Table 1.2: Average Level of Consumption in Rs *Per Capita* Per Year with Estimated Minimum Basic Needs 1967-8

| | Rural | | | Urban | | |
	Actual	Estimated basic needs	Actual/ estimated (percentage)	Actual	Estimated basic needs	Actual/ estimated (percentage)
Food expenditure	357.4	397.9	89.8	410.2	449.0	91.4
Total expenditure	484.8	529.3	91.6	667.9	700.8	95.3

Apart from nutrition, which we consider later, other physical indicators point in a similar direction. For instance, in 1971 the rural literacy rate was 24 per cent against 52 per cent for the urban areas (Government of India Ministry of Information, 1975, p. 52). Less than a third of the allopathic doctors[17] serve the rural population, who constitute 80 per cent of the total (Government of India NSS, 1972, p.3). This means that in terms of all paths the urban areas are eight to nine times better provided than the rural areas. The scarcity resulting from the unwillingness of doctors to practise in rural areas has led to high fees for these doctors in rural areas. According to a sample survey conducted by the NSS, minimum fees charged by these doctors per visit in rural areas were at least 50 per cent higher than in the urban areas (Government of India NSS, 1972, p. 5). As we shall see later, the doctor's fees are beyond the reach of the poor, who are therefore forced largely to depend on charitable dispensaries. However, only 3 per cent of villages have a charitable dispensary within 5 kilometres. Less than 20 per cent of villages have a family planning clinic within a distance of 5km as against 93 per cent for the towns (p.2). Over one-quarter of the villages had no drinking water supply within their own boundaries, although the villages were reasonably well provided with respect to postal and telegraph services, nearly two-thirds of the villages having post and telegraph offices within 5km. However, the villages were poorly provided with facilities for cold storage and fertiliser supply depots; fewer than 3 per cent of villages had cold storage within 5km, and only about 19 per cent a fertiliser depot within 5km (p. 2). By early 1977 only one-third of the villages in India had electricity (Government of India Planning Commission, 1978, p. 164).[18]

Thus it is undeniable that the rural areas come out worse in terms of the provision of amenities as compared with the urban areas. In this respect Lipton's (1977) allegations of 'urban bias' in planning in India certainly have ample justification. One of the main reasons, as Lipton rightly argues, is that decision making is largely in the hands of the urban elite. In a study of the social background of the All-India Administrative Services, it was found that almost 80 per cent of all recruits came from the urban salaried and professional middle class (Subramaniam, 1971, p. 124). Much the same is true of the top echelons of the political hierarchy.

Consumption Levels of the Target Groups

As our earlier discussion showed, very substantial diversity exists among the various estimates of the poverty line in India and hence of the proportion of the population who lie below it. Our designation of the bottom income classes, in both rural and urban areas, as those below the poverty line places approximately one-third of the population in this category. The levels of *per capita* consumption of these target groups are shown, against the all-India average,[19] in Table 1.3.

Table 1.3: Level and Pattern of Consumption of 'Target' Groups: Rural and Urban, 1967-8 (in Rs *per capita*)*

Item	Rural poor		Urban poor		All-India average	
Foodgrains	109.7		111.1		168.2	
Fruits and vegetables	27.5		40.4		52.4	
Livestock products	11.4		25.2		57.6	
Sugar and gur	9.1		10.3		22.9	
Vanaspati and other vegetable oils	10.2		17.9		21.7	
Miscellaneous food products including tea, coffee and tobacco	25.8		26.8		44.9	
Total food	193.7	(78.3)	231.7	(79.2)	367.7	(70.7)
Textiles including footwear and leather goods	6.3		7.6		41.8	
Other manufactures	5.8		7.1		21.6	
Total manufactures	12.1	(4.9)	14.7	(5.0)	63.4	(12.2)
Fuel and light	1.7		2.3		3.8	
Education	0.2		1.6		6.0	
Medical	2.5		4.9		10.3	
Services	37.3		37.4		68.8	
Total other items	41.7	(16.8)	46.2	(15.8)	88.9	(17.1)
Total consumption expenditure	247.5	(100)	292.6	(100)	520.0	(100)
Total disposable income	171.0		234.1		541.9	

Note: *Figures in parentheses are percentages. For groups of items see notes to Table 1.1.
Source: own estimates, as in Table 1.1.

Total consumption expenditure of the rural poor is about 85 per cent of that of the urban poor. However, again, allowance for price differences between the rural and urban areas, and for items such as home-produced vegetables, fruits and meat will reduce the differences. Much the same will be true of total food expenditure. Expenditure on food grains is much the same in both cases; in the case of fruits and vegetables, livestock products and edible oils, a significant part of the higher urban expenditure level can be explained in terms of the proportions domestically produced versus

those purchased for cash. The higher urban expenditure on miscellaneous foods, including tea, coffee, etc. may be the result of urban living
where people, because of their working conditions, may have to eat
more often away from home. Total food expenditure is roughly the
same proportion to total expenditure in both groups — 80 per cent. The
differences between the two groups in other items of consumption are
rather small and probably attributable to differences in prices.

Two very important points emerge from Table 1.3. First, both the
groups cannot meet their consumption expenditure from their disposable incomes, the deficit being somewhat larger for the rural poor as
compared to the urban; on the average they must be dissaving or
incurring debt. It is a well-known description of the rural poor that
they are born in debt, live in debt and die in debt, passing their debt
burden to the next generation. What is not well known is the credit
status of the urban poor, but since most of these remain un- and
underemployed for long periods it is not difficult to visualise them too
living in debt. This evidence on dissaving by the poor, and often by the
middle income groups also, is systematically confirmed from other years
and other surveys, raising the question as to how it is possible for such
substantial groups on the average persistently to obtain the credits
required for a net increase in their indebtedness. Bardhan (1974,
p. 107) makes a substantial contribution to the explanation, pointing
out that, at any time, those with low incomes are likely to be incurring
debt, but owing to the vertical mobility of individuals between income
classes, the composition of the group designated as poor will be
changing; thus the apparent year-to-year increase in the net indebtedness of particular income groups is partly illusory. It is also conceivable
that the income shortfall is partly due to errors of measurement,
income being more likely to be systematically under-recorded than
consumption; evidence, however, has not been adduced to raise this
beyond plausible speculation.[20]

The other significant fact emerges more clearly from Table 1.4,
page 37, which is based on Table 1.3. The disposable income *per
capita* of both the groups is significantly less than half the average for
India as a whole. Their total consumption expenditure is around half
of the country average; in the case of the rural poor it is slightly less,
and for the urban poor slightly more, than half. Total food expenditure
of the two groups varies between half and two-thirds of the all-India
average.

Again, the most striking comparison of all is between the actual
consumption levels of the poor and the estimates of the levels required

for basic needs. It is clear from Table 1.4 that for both groups their average levels of disposable income are sufficient for only one-third of the estimated expenditure necessary to meet their basic needs. Moreover it can meet barely half of the minimum food requirements — 43 per cent for the rural poor, and 52 per cent for the urban poor. Even dissaving is only a very limited offset to the total inadequacy of the income levels.

Table 1.4: Levels of Consumption of 'Target' Groups, Rural and Urban, as Proportion of All-India Average Consumption Levels, 1967-8 (in percentages)

Item	Rural poor	Urban poor
Foodgrains	65.2	66.1
Fruits and vegetables	52.5	77.1
Livestock products	19.8	43.8
Sugar and gur	39.7	45.0
Vanaspati and vegetable oil	47.0	82.5
Miscellaneous food products including tea, coffee and tobacco	57.5	60.0
Total food	52.7	63.0
Textiles including footwear and leather goods	15.1	18.2
Other manufactures	26.8	32.9
Total manufactures	19.1	23.2
Fuel and light	45.2	61.1
Education	3.3	26.6
Medical	24.2	47.5
Services	41.9	42.1
Total other items	46.9	52.0
Total consumption expenditure	47.6	56.3
Total disposable income	31.6	43.2
Total disposable income as proportion of basic minimum needs expenditure	32.3/43.0[a]	33.4/52.1[a]

[a]Total disposable income as a proportion of the basic needs *food* expenditure only. For groups of items see notes to Table 1.1, page 32.
Source: Tables 1.2 and 1.3.

Marginal Expenditure Patterns

Marginal consumption patterns reveal the harsh realities of the inadequacy of the income and consumption levels of the poor with similar force.[21] Of every increase in the income of the rural poor 97 per cent goes on consumption expenditure, as against only 56 per cent for the rural rich[22] (Table 1.5). Food purchases take 89 per cent and grain alone 41 per cent of the increase in consumption. So little is left after spending on food that the rural poor can spend only about 8 per cent of their marginal rupee on manufactures and only 3 per cent on all services, including transport, education, medical services and entertainment. The situation is much the same for the urban poor. With a marginal propensity to consume of 0.95 they again scarcely save. Of their

Table 1.5: Marginal Consumer's Expenditure per Re Increase in Disposable Income, 1967-8, Rs (percentages in parentheses)[a]

Item	Rural			Urban		
	Bottom	Middle	Top	Bottom	Middle	Top
1. Rice	0.176	0.086	0.025	0.037	0.014	0.003
2. Wheat	0.074	0.055	0.016	0.072	0.025	0.006
3. Pulses	0.080	0.032	0.011	0.005	0.001	0.0003
4. Other foodgrains	0.072	0.017	0.003	0.013	0.0006	-0.0001
5. Total foodgrains	0.402	0.190	0.055	0.127	0.041	0.009
	(41.3)	(24.8)	(9.8)	(13.4)	(5.2)	(1.5)
6. Fruits and vegetables	0.139	0.059	0.025	0.184	0.082	0.045
7. Other agriculture	0.012	0.003	0.0006	0.002	0.0001	—
8. Livestock products, etc.	0.115	0.102	0.084	0.181	0.127	0.088
9. Sugar and gur	0.078	0.042	0.027	0.033	0.012	0.004
10. Vanaspati and other vegetable oils	0.072	0.033	0.011	0.098	0.045	0.020
11. Cigarettes & tobacco	0.008	0.002	0.0005	0.028	0.012	0.0015
12. Miscellaneous food including tea and coffee	0.037	0.018	0.013	0.063	0.031	0.024
13. Total food	0.863	0.449	0.216	0.716	0.350	0.192
	(88.6)	(58.6)	(38.6)	(75.7)	(44.8)	(31.8)
14. Textiles including footwear and leather products	0.051	0.047	0.044	0.052	0.045	0.029
15. Other manufactures	0.026	0.014	0.030	0.044	0.025	0.070
16. Total manufactures	0.077	0.061	0.074	0.096	0.070	0.099
	(7.9)	(8.0)	(13.2)	(10.1)	(9.0)	(16.3)
17. Fuel and light	0.006	0.002	0.002	0.008	0.005	0.004
18. Education	0.002	0.006	0.007	0.022	0.031	0.036
19. Medicine	0.019	0.010	0.007	0.039	0.022	0.016
20. Services	0.003	0.235	0.253	0.064	0.304	0.258
21. Total other sectors	0.030	0.253	0.269	0.133	0.362	0.314
	(3.1)	(33.0)	(48.0)	(14.1)	(46.3)	(51.7)
22. Total consumption[b]	0.974	0.766	0.560	0.946	0.782	0.607
	(100)	(100)	(100)	(100)	(100)	(100)

[a]Marginal expenditures are estimated at each group's mean income from expenditure functions fitted to NSS and NCAER data. For rural and urban expenditure elasticities, see Table 1.6, page 39. For details of groups of items, see notes to Table 1.1, page 32.

[b]Totals do not add because of rounding error and also because small miscellaneous items are not included.

marginal consumption 76 per cent is spent on food, a significantly lower proportion than for the rural poor, due to the subsidised but rationed distribution of grain through the 'fair price' shops. Correspondingly, they spend rather more than the rural poor on manufactures and substantially more on education, transport and other services.

For purposes of comparison the marginal expenditure patterns of the middle and top groups are also shown in Table 1.5. Food purchases, and particularly grains, diminish rapidly in importance as income rises, while services increase clearly between the bottom and middle income groups, but then less markedly. Strikingly, purchases of manufactures are never large; while they increase significantly in terms of their share in the marginal rupee of expenditure, the marginal propensity to consume them, per rupee of income, is very stable.

The critically low level of living of the poor is further emphasised when the concept of a 'luxury' is applied. A good is conventionally defined to be a luxury when the income elasticity of demand for it exceeds unity. Table 1.6 shows that for the rural bottom group all of the selected items except 'other food grains' (the so-called 'inferior' grains, such as barley and millet) and, marginally, rice are luxuries with expenditure elasticities[23] typically greater than unity. Similarly,

Table 1.6: Expenditure Elasticities of Selected Items, 1967-8

		Rural			Urban	
Item	Bottom	Middle	Top	Bottom	Middle	Top
Rice	0.96	0.56	0.30	0.24	0.12	0.06
Wheat	1.67	0.97	0.53	0.77	0.40	0.19
Pulses	1.31	0.76	0.41	1.15	0.60	0.29
Other foodgrains	0.47	0.24	0.10	0.18	0.05	-0.02
Fruits and nuts	2.49	1.36	0.65	3.72	2.03	1.06
Vegetables	1.34	0.83	0.51	1.50	0.93	0.61
Milk	2.95	1.89	1.22	2.39	1.53	1.04
Meat, fish and eggs	1.89	1.15	0.69	1.89	1.13	0.70
Sugar	2.55	1.55	0.93	1.31	0.81	0.53
Gur	2.06	1.26	0.76	0.81	0.38	0.13
Vanaspati	3.62	1.91	0.83	2.85	1.50	0.72
Other oils	1.44	0.90	0.56	1.45	0.90	0.59
Miscellaneous food products	1.22	0.79	0.51	1.59	1.07	0.77
Cotton textiles	2.10	1.17	0.59	2.68	1.37	0.63
Footwear	4.35	2.38	1.15	4.11	2.05	0.87
Education	2.42	1.25	0.52	3.47	1.87	0.95
Medical expenses	2.26	1.27	0.65	3.38	1.84	0.96

Source: These elasticities of item expenditure with respect to total expenditure were estimated from expenditure functions fitted to NSS and NCAER data, using a variety of functional forms (log-inverse, log-log-inverse, power function). The figures in the table were evaluated at 1967-8 income group mean expenditure levels.

for the urban bottom group all of the items except rice, wheat, the inferior grains and gur are luxuries; and even the elasticities for rice and wheat may be artificially low because of the rationing of these foods through 'fair price' shops. If this is the case, then most items of consumption are luxuries for both the rural and the urban poor.[24] This is clearly not so for the rural and urban top groups, while the middle income groups purchase a number of major food items with elasticities less than unity.

Nutritional Status of the Target Groups

The luxury status of most foods, and the serious shortfall of both disposable income and consumption from the expenditure on food estimated as necessary for basic needs, suggest that severe malnutrition is inevitable among the poor.

Recent diet surveys throw significant light on the nutritional state of the 'target' groups. These surveys have been conducted mainly in rural areas, particularly among poor peasants, agricultural labourers, handicraft workers,[25] etc. It is clear from Table 1.7 that on the all-India level these families did not meet their calorie requirements, although their protein requirement was invariably met. In most of the poorer states (Bihar, Kerala, Madras, Rajasthan, and West Bengal) the average calorie intake was lower than the all-India average and significantly lower than the Indian Council of Medical Research (ICMR) — even FAO — recommendations. On a disaggregated level the situation was sometimes more critical. For instance, although the average calorie intake in Bihar is

Table 1.7: Nutritional Status of Rural Poor, 1967-8 (*per capita*)

State	Calories	Protein (g)	Fats (g)
Andhra	2,311	57.7	29.5
Bihar	1,830	53.3	15.8
Kerala	1,833	45.0	26.0
Madras	1,392	39.2	12.5
Punjab	2,974	89.6	57.3
Rajasthan	1,986	68.0	32.6
UP	2,414	73.7	35.0
West Bengal	1,749	39.6	23.8
All states	2,061	58.3	29.1
ICMR recommendation	2,400	44.55	

Source: ICMR (1967, pp. 16-17). The families covered, though predominantly poor, do not exactly correspond to our rural poor.

reported in Table 1.7 at 1,830, several surveys reported between 1,600 and 1,700 calories; in one case the figure was as low as 1,283. In the case of Madras the lowest was 961, for Rajasthan 1,123 and for West Bengal around 1,600.

In years of drought the levels of calorie intake go down much further (ICMR, 1967, pp. 20-79). Then landless labourers and subsistence farmers face not only a shortfall in their own production but also a drastic reduction in employment opportunities on large farms. Thus in the event of a serious drought (or flood) the very poor in rural areas suffer from a double squeeze; their purchasing power goes down because of their poor crops, at a time when the price of their purchases tends to rise because of a decline in the supply of grains. The problem of shortage is often aggravated by speculative hoarding by traders. Evidence from drought-stricken areas of India suggests that calorie intake may in such situations fall to little more than a quarter of the requirement (Casley, Simaika and Sinha, 1974).

In most developing countries, the rural poor tend to fare slightly better than the urban poor from a nutritional standpoint (United Nations FAO, 1975, p. 14). This is true of India as well. In the Fourth World Food Survey (United Nations FAO, 1977, p. 56) FAO estimate for 1971/2 it was shown that 21 per cent of the rural households received less than 2,100 calories per adult consumer unit,[26] while the corresponding figure for urban areas was around 24 per cent. After adjusting for the differences in household size, in the lowest income groups 49.5 per cent of rural households received less than 1.2 BMR whereas among urban households the percentage was as high as 70.2. In the next income group (Rs 25-43) the corresponding figures were 8.9 per cent (rural) and 26.9 per cent (urban) (United Nations FAO, 1977, pp. 56, 58).

These deficiencies in the nutritional standards of the poor are repeated in many other aspects of their quality of life. With regard to housing conditions, little information is available but it is well known that both the rural and urban poor live in atrocious conditions.[27]

It does not take much imagination to see that these groups, particularly in rural areas, can have few resources to meet the medical and educational needs of their families. According to the NSS, the minimum fee per visit for an allopath in rural areas was around Rs 8 (Government of India NSS, 1972, p. 12) which would be equivalent to expenditure on foodgrains for one person for 26 days. A midwife's minimum delivery fee in rural areas was reported to be around Rs 7 (p. 12). In urban areas the doctor's fee came to be around Rs 5.2

(p. 17) which could buy one person's foodgrains for nearly 17 days. Some of these people, obviously, would go to a charitable dispensary or government hospital, but many of these, particularly in rural areas, are permanently understaffed and are short of medicines. In practical terms, medical attention is typically a luxury for both the rural and the urban poor.

The situation with education is unquestionably better, particularly for the harijans and the other Backward Classes and the Scheduled Tribes. For these groups there are special reservations in schools and colleges together with provisions for scholarships. But various studies point out that the spread of education among the Scheduled Castes and Tribes has been rather slow. The general consensus is that only a small subelite has benefited from such schemes, while the large majority of these groups have lagged behind.[28] In spite of the quotas in various government jobs, their share in various services continues to be rather marginal. This is not only true of the Scheduled Tribes and the Scheduled Castes but also of the 'sons of the poorer farmers, artisans, and industrial workers' (Subramaniam, 1971, p. 126).[29]

The difficulties involved in ensuring basic minimum needs to the poor of India are obviously immense. The basic minimum for everyone cannot be achieved even with complete equality in the distribution of incomes and regardless of the consequences. In this sense distributional equality is tantamount to 'sharing poverty'.[30] The enormity even of the economic problem is intimidating. And the economic problem cannot, except for analytical purposes, be separated from its social and political context, and ensuring basic needs in that sphere requires bringing about changes in the social and psychological attitudes of both the privileged and the underprivileged.

Since one of the fundamental determinants of the status of the poor is their income levels the exploration of these, both their origins and their implications, seems an obvious point of entry into the analysis of the more narrowly economic aspects of the problem. Our specific approach is to construct a macro-model with the conventional income-expenditure-output framework but explicitly integrating into this the distribution of incomes, by income class. It is to this task that we now turn.

Notes

1. See also Streeten and Burki (1977), ILO (1977), Lisk (1977), Lisk and Werneke (1976) and Hopkins (1977).

2. *Constituent Assembly Debates* (CAD), II, 3, 316, quoted in Austin (1966, p. 26).

3. K. Santhanam, in magazine section of *The Hindustan Times* (1946), quoted in Austin (1966, p. 26).

4. It would be wrong to imply that Nehru was the only person who favoured the idea of a planned economy. Many other leaders of the Indian National Congress had preached the virtues of planning as early as the late 1920s (Austin, 1966, p.235). Prominent industrialists and bankers themselves were not opposed to the idea of economic planning and produced in 1945 a plan which came to be known as the 'Bombay Plan'. Some Indian Marxist leaders wrote a 'People's Plan'. The Gandhian economists had produced a 'Gandhian Plan'.

5. Mahatma Gandhi, in an interview with foreign correspondents at Mussorie in 1946, quoted in Panikkar (1963, p. 184).

6. As Austin indicates, although the 'ideal of a revived village life with benevolent panchayats and decentralised government bringing democracy to the grass-roots level appealed to Assembly members', in order to reconcile the needs for maintaining unity and stability, together with economic and social change, they decided in favour of a 'non-traditional' constitution, with a tendency towards 'centralization' (Austin, 1966, pp. 31-2).

7. The Planning Commission of India as early as 1956 had indicated that 'in spite of concerted efforts for the mobilisation of available resources and their optimum utilisation as proposed in the second plan, the impact on the two-fold problem of unemployment and under-employment will not be as large as the situation demands'. See Government of India Planning Commission (1956, p. 124).

8. For the detail of the various estimates and discussion see Bardhan (1974). Minhas (1970) and Vaidyanathan (1974) adopt the Planning Commission estimates. See also Minhas (1974).

9. *The Eastern Economist*, Budget Number, 17 March (1978), and Government of India Planning Commission (1978, p. 3).

10. This estimate is based on the NSS 1971-2 data.

11. Generalisation in this respect along caste lines is often risky. The socio-economic conditions of the various castes differ substantially between regions. In many parts of North India, Brahmins, though highest in the social hierarchy, are often the poorest groups, living on alms. Many of them serve as cooks to well-to-do families of other castes; their economic status may often be worse than domestic servants of 'lower castes', as the female members of the lower caste will accept domestic service while Brahmin women, for social reasons, will not accept domestic positions other than as a cook. Many caste groups included in the official list of 'backward classes' may, in many areas, be more prosperous than their higher caste counterparts. As a result of the special constitutional privileges to backward classes there is a clamour to be classified as 'backward'. A Backward Class Commission, set up in 1953 to compile a list of castes to be treated as economically and socially backward, admitted the claim of 'backwardness' of 239 communities in addition to the *harijans* (untouchables) and the tribal population. In all, these amounted to almost three-quarters of the total Indian population. See Srinivas (1962, p. 40).

12. Since the increasing importance of modern technology in agriculture has led to increasing self-cultivation there is a growing tendency to carry out such evictions. On the basis of a detailed survey of 275 randomly selected villages in West Bengal, Bihar and some of the eastern districts of Uttar Pradesh (UP), Bardhan and Rudra show that 'The overwhelming majority of villages where

tenant eviction is reported to be increasing are advanced or highly advanced. Apart from increased profitability of self-cultivation preventive action in the face of protective tenancy legislation has obviously motivated increased tenant eviction on the part of landlords' (Bardhan and Rudra, 1978, p. 381).

13. These estimates are not directly comparable with the NSS *per capita* consumption because the aggregate data is based on Central Statistical Organisation (CSO) estimates and the distributor between income groups is based on the relevant data from the NSS. Since all the details required were not available from the same NSS round, several rounds had to be used, as well as data from the National Council of Applied Economic Research (NCAER). We are aware of the limitations of this methodology (see, for instance, Bardhan, (1974, pp. 124-5)); some bias may be introduced into the shares of consumption as the NSS probably underestimate the consumption of both the very rich and the very poor, but it is difficult to see which way the net bias will be.

14. Accounting for fuel and light, particularly for the rural areas, faces the same kinds of problems as fruits and vegetables or livestock products, for most of the fuel in rural areas is collected by the villagers themselves and it is not easy to impute values for these.

15. The above results conform broadly to the NSS data for the 22nd round.

16. Obviously, for physically more arduous work or for non-vegetarians recommendations would be higher. For further details see Kadekodi (1978).

17. 'Allopathic doctor' in India refers to doctors trained in 'Western' medicine, largely on British lines. In addition to the allopaths, there is a large number of homoeopaths, *vaids* and *hakims* practising other systems of medicine. If allowance is made for them there is 1 doctor per 2,250 persons in the rural areas and 1 for every 570 persons in the urban areas. Since there are significant quality differences among these groups, such averages may be deceptive. On the other hand, contrary to general belief, some doctors practising indigenous medicine are well qualified, and to consider them 'inferior' to the allopaths may be unjust. See Jeffrey (1978).

18. It ought, however, to be pointed out that even in the People's Republic of China, in spite of the egalitarian ideology, such significant inequities between rural and urban areas have emerged. It was for this reason that, since the Cultural Revolution, reducing the rural-urban imbalance has become one of the major policies; but many of the imbalances still persist.

19. While our interest here is to analyse the levels of consumption of the 'target' groups on an all-India level, it is important to remember that the 'target' groups will probably have an even more difficult existence in poorer areas. Bhatty found that in 1968/9 Gujarat, Tamil Nadu, Madhya Pradesh, Rajasthan and Orissa were the poorest states of India. In each of these states between 80 and 84 per cent of people had incomes below his estimate of the poverty line at Rs 360 per year (1974, pp. 325-6). Dandekar and Rath (1971a) suggest the following states as having the largest populations below the poverty line: Kerala (90.75%), Andhra Pradesh (62.14%), Maharastra (61.04%), Tamil Nadu (55.19%). According to them Gujarat and Rajasthan had rather low figures. For a more recent study on regional aspects of Indian poverty see Majmudar (1977). See also Farbman (1974), Ahluwalia (1978).

20. For further information and discussions of savings in India, see Rudra (1972), Roy (1975), Government of India CSO (1969) and NCAER (1972).

21. Marginal patterns will be crucial to the responses of consumption to income changes in the simulations with the complete model.

22. This, perhaps surprisingly, low figure must be seen in the context of the discussion above on the extent of dissaving by the poor. Every debt incurred implies the accumulation of a corresponding asset by a creditor; in rural areas sales of land and agricultural assets form an important part of this process.

Besides, the rural rich are known to keep liquid assets for speculative purposes, including substantial hoards of gold in one form or another. Furthermore, where social ceremonial expenditure (marriages, dowries, etc.) have a high correlation with status in the social hierarchy, a high saving propensity may be understandable.

23. Expenditure elasticities are typically somewhat less than income elasticities.

24. This is consistent with other results obtained by various researchers. For instance, Sinha and Hay (1972) found that the income elasticity for cereals and pulses as well as total food for agricultural labourers was greater than unity. See also Iyengar and Jain (1974), Gupta (1973).

25. In some cases such as Andhra Pradesh, Uttar Pradesh and Punjab, incomes were beyond the levels corresponding to our rural poor.

26. Based on Indian age structure one person roughly equals 0.85 adult consumer unit.

27. For some information on average number of persons per room see Planning Commission (1969, Part II, p. 14), also Ganguli and Gupta (1976, pp. 65-75). Because of the enormous quality differential between houses such indices have little value.

28. On this see Ahmad (1978), Chitnis (1972), Duskin (1972), Floud (1975), Patwardhan (1973), Singh (1977), Sinha (1977) and Schermerhorn (1978).

29. There is one genuinely economic problem. As Bhagwati points out, for the poor there is a high opportunity cost in sending children to school since they could work and add to the family income. Furthermore, employment opportunities for the poor, particularly in the rural areas, are rather limited and therefore the private rate of return to primary education is rather low. In addition, if primary education assists in increasing the agricultural productivity of labour, little advantage will accrue to landless labour in the absence of land. Bhagwati argues that genuine equality of educational opportunities will continue to be elusive for a long time (Bhagwati, 1973, p. 36). See also Sher (1975, p. 165).

30. Sinha has argued elsewhere that for eliminating or at least minimising misery and deprivation, 'sharing of poverty' may be a social necessity. In fact, in the People's Republic of China, it has, by improving the well-being of the people and thereby their sense of participation, increased the overall productive capacity of the country substantially (Sinha, 1976, pp. 46, 127). As will be seen later, we do simulate the effects of a radical land redistribution and also complete equality but the parameters are changed so drastically that we consider our results highly speculative. Besides, on political grounds we do not think such radical changes are feasible, at least not in the short run.

2 A MACRO-ECONOMIC MODEL OF INCOME DISTRIBUTION

Our broad objective is to model, in a macro-economic context, the process of income generation and distribution particularly as it affects those socio-economic groups below a poverty line. By tracing the sources of the incomes of the various groups we aim to be able to simulate the impact on the distribution of incomes and on the position of target groups of a variety of possible developments or policies: income transfers between groups, alternative growth patterns, and changes in the economic structure.

Since the distribution of personal incomes is largely determined by the pattern of factor earnings in production, and in turn affects the level and pattern of expenditure, the basic framework for the model is the conventional macro-economic circular flow of income through the income-expenditure-output sequence. But the incorporation of distributional aspects involves important extensions of the consistency requirements of the standard macro-framework. In particular, any distribution of incomes among socio-economic groups implies a particular sectoral pattern of expenditure and so of production; and as individual groups derive their incomes in differing proportions from the various production sectors, any pattern of output gives rise to a particular distribution of incomes generated. Of the many patterns of income distribution, therefore, which might be considered as policy targets, only a limited set will be consistent with the distribution created by their expenditure pattern. Any others will be feasible only with sustained fiscal intervention.

These consistency aspects involved in the distribution of incomes impose major requirements on the structure of the model on both the income and expenditure sides. On the incomes side, the distribution of personal incomes must be explicitly derived from the profile of incomes generated by production in each sector. In thus 'closing the loop' or including 'the final iteration' into the income-expenditure sequence we aim to overcome the major limitation of much earlier work in this area, emphasised in the survey by Morawetz (1974, pp. 504-6).

The differing shares of the respective groups in value added by sector are, moreover, an important channel through which alternative growth strategies affect the distribution of incomes. The allocation of value added among classes at the sectoral level thus not only is a key element for the analysis of income distribution in its static aspects, but also provides an avenue of approach to the integrated analysis of income distribution and growth.

Incorporation of the full implications of income distribution requires that groups be distinguished with reference not only to their position in the economic structure as income recipients but also to their behaviour on the expenditure side. This involves the identification of groups at varying income levels and in differing socio-economic circumstances, where these will have a significant impact on their consumption patterns. In addition to this, concern with the position of the poorest groups relative to their basic needs prompts the demarcation of the classes in a way which at least approximately identifies those below the poverty line.

The differing commodity patterns of expenditure of groups at different income levels and their implications, through production, for factor use have been made the basis for an extensive discussion of the employment potential of income redistribution, following ILO (1970, 1971). The major role of unemployment and underemployment in the poverty problem prompts the incorporation in our model of the employment implications of production alongside the income distribution generated.

The final consideration which has had a significant impact on the general structure of our model derives from the more narrowly technical issue of the form adopted for the expenditure functions for the individual commodities. Since the importance of income distribution on the expenditure side, and in particular for its employment potential, lies in the assumption that the pattern of consumption expenditure differs significantly across income classes, we have rejected the various standard forms of expenditure function which imply constancy in the marginal propensity to consume or the consumption elasticity of individual commodities, in favour of more general forms which allow these to vary with the level of income; these forms are typically non-linear in income. The price of this flexibility between the consumption propensity and income is that the model as a whole becomes non-linear, with the consequent loss of the direct or analytical solution through matrix inversion and the need to achieve a numerical solution through iterative procedures. The solution sequence adopted, of iteration round the circular flow, of itself contributes useful insights into the adjustment processes involved, for incomes, output and expenditure, following a change at any point in the sequence.

Our model has therefore been developed with the objective of replicating the leading features of the process of income generation and distribution in India. The model is based on the standard macro-economic framework of the simultaneous determination of output, expenditure and income, but augmented by the disaggregation of personal incomes by socio-economic class, both as generated by the sectoral structure of production and as determinants of the pattern of consumption expenditure. It provides a conceptual and numerical framework through which we can analyse the sources of the existing income distribution, the impact of hypothetical changes in the distribution, and the distributional implications of alternative growth strategies.

The form in which any model is finally estimated typically represents a compromise between its designers' objectives and the available data. Somewhat surprisingly, in our case the limitations imposed from the data side have not, as far as model structure is concerned, been as great as might be expected. While we in no way wish to suggest that we had to hand all the appropriate data, where the implementation of our model has been curtailed this has usually been primarily for conceptual reasons or in order deliberately to limit its scope, rather than for lack of data. The problems of inadequate coverage, and of incompatibilities and inconsistencies among data from different sources − or even from the same source − have been enormous, as would be expected with the importance of subsistence production and the informal sector for the issues we are treating; but we have adopted the general strategy of trying to make the maximum use of even fragmentary data, and excluding desirable features of the model only as a last resort.

Structure of the Model

Heuristic insight into the structure of the model can be gained from its representation in terms of the circular flow of income. This is illustrated in the flow chart (Figure 2.1, page 49) where the lines with arrows trace the income flows through the main economic processes of expenditure, production, the creation of value added and the distribution of personal incomes. Personal incomes as distributed across socio-economic classes are divided, according to the consumption propensities of the various groups, between consumption expenditure, detailed by commodity, and personal savings. Consumption expenditure combined with the other, exogenous, elements of final demand takes up the outputs of the production sector. The production process engages factors of production, generating both employment and factor incomes. Factor incomes are divided into the after-tax incomes of the personal sector, on the one hand, and government and corporate incomes on the other. Personal incomes, as distributed across socio-economic classes by the production process and modified by the tax system, continue in the circular flow, to generate consumption expenditure. Non-personal incomes give rise to corporate and government savings which, together with the savings of the personal sector, form the total savings of the economy which can be checked, outside the model, against the capital requirements implicit in the production pattern.

Figure 2.1: Circular Flow Chart showing Income Flows Through Main Economic Processes

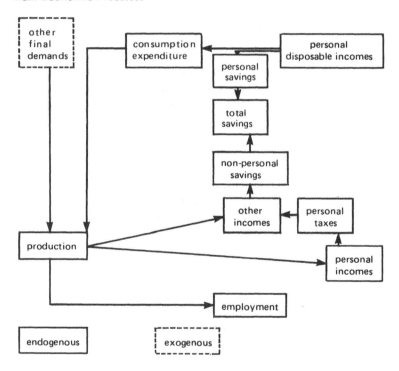

For the base year for our study, 1967-8, the figures used for all the constituent elements are the actual values for India in that year, adjusted to ensure numerical consistency throughout the model. At these values the flow of income through the system is self-replicating and we accept this as an equilibrium or solution of the model.

In the aggregate, of course, expenditure, production and income generation are continuous and simultaneous processes and are appropriately represented as simultaneously determined. In these terms the model is a semi-closed Leontief system, semi-closed in that one of the elements of final demand, consumption expenditure, is endogenously determined through the level and distribution of personal incomes arising from the process of production. Applications of closed Leontief models in this area are rare, however, while the open model has been used on a number of occasions as a framework for assessing the impact of income redistribution on employment. A brief discussion of the open model may therefore be useful in setting the context for the partial closure incorporated in our variant.

The standard formulation of the open Leontief model of the determination of employment has the basic flow equations

$$X = AX + F \dotfill (1a)$$

where X and F are, respectively, column vectors of gross output and final demand by industry, and A the matrix of technical coefficients relating each industry's input use to its gross output. When the vector(s) of final demands are determined exogenously then

$$X = (I\text{-}A)^{-1}F \dotfill (1b)$$

where $(I\text{-}A)^{-1}F$ is the standard Leontief inverse coefficient matrix. When, in keeping with the Leontief methodology, employment in each industry is related to its gross output by a fixed coefficient, the implications of the model for total employment, N, follow

$$N = eX \dotfill (1c)$$

where e is a row vector of the number of persons employed per unit of gross output. The model then yields estimates of the employment implications of alternative distributions of personal incomes when these, and their associated consumption patterns, are generated outside the model.[1]

The most interesting application of a model of this type relevant in the present context is by the Government of India Planning Commission (1973). As part of the planning exercise associated with the preparation of the Fifth Plan they made projections of two alternative sets of final demand vectors, the first for given growth rates of GDP incorporating the distribution of consumption expenditure which they would imply with no intervention, and the second with consumption expenditure redistributed such that the poorest 30 per cent of the population, who would otherwise be below the poverty line, would be raised to the minimum subsistence level. They then simulated the implications of these for GDP and other macro-indices, but not for employment. With redistribution of consumption the rates of growth of consumption expenditure in the poorer groups would be much higher than the average, with the top groups experiencing an actual reduction in their absolute level of consumption expenditure, while without redistribution the consumption of all groups would grow at approximately equal rates. Traced through to the sectoral level, redistribution would involve higher rates of growth of output of essential commodities such as foodgrains, other agriculture and cotton textiles, and reduced growth rates for a number of manufactured products. Broadly similar models have been applied in a number of developing countries of Asia and Latin America to examine the impact on output and employment of income redistribution in either its static or its dynamic aspects.[2]

The main problem implied in the use of the open Leontief framework in this context is one of consistency. The vector of gross outputs by industry is, by construction, consistent with the pattern of final demand, but because of the 'open' structure of the model, i.e. the exogenous determination of final demands, there is no mechanism which ensures reciprocal consistency between the structure of personal incomes generated by the industry gross outputs and the various final demand vectors proposed. This consistency can be achieved, notionally, only by effecting whatever fiscal transfers are required to adjust the discrepancy between the pattern of personal incomes generated and the proposed distribution.

To ensure this consistency and incorporate the feedback from the distribution of incomes generated to the pattern of consumption expenditure, our model incorporates two significant extensions to the standard format of the open Leontief system, one affecting the expenditures (row) and the other the purchases (column) aspect of the system. On the income side the conventional two rows representing the functional distribution of value added between wages and profits, as the payments to the factors labour and capital, are first elaborated into various categories of factor income, differentiated by the institutional status of the recipient, and then translated into personal incomes, distinguished by socio-economic group, and non-personal incomes. Since this two-stage procedure is described in detail below, for the present discussion we will telescope it into the replacement of the wage and profit rows by a series of rows, one for the personal income of each class and one for non-personal incomes. On the expenditure side, in order to incorporate the differing characteristics of the consumption patterns of the various socio-economic classes, the vector of personal consumption expenditure is subdivided into a set of vectors for each class. The consumption vector for each group is determined by its level of disposable income, its gross personal income as generated from production less the direct tax taken into non-personal incomes.

The flow structure of the model as augmented in these terms is shown in Table 2.1 In the conventional manner the flows of output are represented across the rows of the table and purchases down the columns.

Table 2.1: Flow Structure of the Model

		Purchases by industry $l.\ldots\ldots j.\ldots\ldots n$	Consumption by class $l..k..m$	Other final demand	Total sales
Sales by industry	l $.$ $.$ $.$ $.$ $.$ i $.$ $.$ $.$ $.$ $.$ n	Zone I X_{ij}	Zone III C_{ik}	OF_i	X_l $.$ $.$ X_i $.$ $.$ X_n
Value added by class	l $.$ $.$ k $.$ $.$ $m+l$	Y_{ll} Zone II Y_{ln} Y_{kj}	Zone IV O		Y_l $.$ Y_k $.$ Y_{m+l}
Total Purchases		$X_l \ldots X_j \ldots X_n$	$C_l..C_k..C_m$ OF		

Zone I is the normal interindustry flow table where the typical element X_{ij} represents, in its row connotation, the output of industry i sold to industry j and, equivalently, in its column connotation the purchase by industry j of the output of industry i. Zone II comprises the elements of value added by industry, differentiated by socio-economic class. Typical element Y_{kj} represents the income accruing to class k from the employment of factors, labour or capital, which it owns, by industry j. All but the last of the classes receive personal incomes, the last class containing non-personal (corporate and government) income. Zone III contains the final demands, consumption expenditure distinguished by socio-economic class, and other final demand; the typical consumption element C_{ik} represents consumption of the output of industry i by class k, as determined by its level of personal income Y_k, while other final demand OF_i is regarded as exogenous. Zone IV contains only zero elements by definition, since all purchases which final users make directly from value added, such as domestic services, are classified into the production sectors. The row total X_i represents the gross output of industry i as the sum of the flows to all intermediate and final users. Row total Y_k represents the total disposable income received by class k from all production activities.

The flow equations for the augmented model are therefore

$$X = AX + C(Y) + OF. \dotfill (2a)$$
$$Y = VX \dotfill (2b)$$
$$N = eX \dotfill (2c)$$

with notation as before and V the matrix of value added coefficients representing the disposable income received by each class per unit of gross output in each industry. In a fully linear model the $(n+m+1)$ flow equations can be solved, by inversion of a partitioned matrix, for consistent values of industry gross outputs and class incomes, and the associated levels of consumption and employment, for given levels of other final demand.[3]

Several closed Leontief models of broadly this form have been estimated in studies of income distribution in recent years. The most extensive elaboration of the conceptual framework, in terms of a social accounting matrix (SAM) is by Pyatt and Thorbecke (1976); this is made operational for Sri Lanka in Pyatt, Roe and Associates (1977). Before this, however, a very similar model, although not couched in SAM form, had been developed by Weisskoff and applied to the

employment problems of the enclave economy of Puerto Rico
(Weisskoff, 1976, circulated earlier as 1973; Weisskoff and Wolff,
1977). Ballentine and Soligo (1978) report a model developed with an
impressive degree of articulation but estimated on somewhat preliminary data for Colombia as an outgrowth from a USAID project; their
particular objective is to test the hypothesis that the poor tend to consume goods and services produced with factors of production owned
primarily by the poor while the rich consume those produced by factors owned primarily by the rich. Of more limited scope is the study by
Tokman (1975) for Ecuador which concentrates on the employment
effect of income distribution in industrial sectors only. All these models
are linear throughout.[4]

In our model, however, the expenditure functions by commodity
and class, $C(Y)$, are non-linear in class income; consequently the model
solution is obtained iteratively, the sequence of the solution programme
replicating the circular flow of income outlined above. For our base year
the data values have been adjusted to consistency such that the solution
programme derives a circular flow of income which is self-replicating at
these values. Intervention in the model at appropriate points is then
used to simulate hypothetical developments or policies, new solution
values obtaining when the circular flow is again self-replicating, at a new
level and in a new configuration. In our various simulations, conver-
gence has always been obtained, usually rapidly, with the model typically approaching close to the eventual equilibrium values in less than
ten iterations. The impact of the hypothetical changes is then assessed
by the comparison of the final levels of incomes and employment with
their base values.

Designation of Socio-economic Classes

In discussions of the distribution of income a number of different
criteria are used in the designation of economic classes. The traditional
focus of interest in distributional questions has been in the distribution
of national income between the aggregate factors of production, labour
and capital. This approach, which also features in many of the current
models of economic growth, has its counterpart, in the planning context, in the division of value added between wages and profits in a
typical Leontief system. An alternative scheme for the distribution of
income is on an institutional basis, distinguishing the personal or household, corporate and government sectors. A distribution among these
categories is a not uncommon by-product of development planning as it
corresponds directly to categories conventionally used in the compila-

tion of the national income accounts. Both the factor share and the institutional approach, however, are not helpful for approaching the distributional issues which are our central concern, namely poverty and inequality. For these the relevant concept is the size distribution of personal incomes.

Except for transfer payments, personal incomes are received in payment for the use in production of the factor inputs which the individual owns, capital, land and labour, including entrepreneurship and the various forms of human capital. Full articulation of the generation of the distribution of personal incomes from production would appropriately involve a two-stage process: firstly the allocation of the value added of each industry among factor inputs, with labour in particular disaggregated to differentiate payments for the various constituent elements; and secondly the mapping of the factor payments into the distribution of personal incomes by economic or socio-economic class. The appropriate basis for the designation of classes would then be wealth, broadly defined to refer to the stocks of all productive factors and hence earning opportunities which the individual commands. This approach would give an explicit synthesis of the position of socio-economic classes in respect of personal incomes and poverty with their position in terms of the ownership of wealth and income-earning opportunities.

Adequate implementation of this approach raises complex concept-ual as well as practical problems in the measurement of wealth in terms of actual or potential factor inputs. Since our study is the first attempt at this level, certainly for India and indeed for almost any country, to derive the distribution of personal incomes from value added in the production sectors, full representation of this is beyond its scope.[5] But although the distribution of wealth or factors is not formally made the basis of income payments the concept underlies our derivation of the distribution at many points. In agricultural incomes wages and crop incomes are distinguished, with the income class bounds for the latter set on the basis of landholdings. In non-agricultural sectors the broad categories of factor incomes, notably wages, profits and the income of the self-employed, are often distinguished, and the allocation built up through them separately.[6] Moreover, the types of descriptive epithet which the full approach might employ, such as landless labour or un-skilled labour, are useful for the characterisation of groups constituted on other grounds.

We have chosen to demarcate our classes on the basis of income levels, as the best single link between status in production on the one hand and living standard on the other. Income received has the limitation of revealing only the proximate and not the fundamental sources of poverty, which lie in lack of wealth and access to earning opportunities; and because of the intervention of transfers it does not match exactly to status in production. On the other side the level of household income is correlated, but significantly less than perfectly, with the standard of life which is relevant for the delineation of poverty. We have therefore supplemented the classification into income classes by distinguishing the rural and urban populations separately. These populations derive their incomes in very different proportions from the different sectors, and the extent of their ownership of particular categories of wealth, particularly land and skills, is of varying importance for their economic status. On the consumption side also the income equivalent to the subsistence minimum tends to vary systematically between rural and urban areas.[7]

The optimum number of income classes for an exercise such as ours is not a clear-cut issue. The minimum approach is to distinguish two only, those above and those below the poverty line. But the clear focus on poverty which this gives is gained at the cost of a loss of detail in other respects. More than a small number of classes, on the other hand, tends to result in a loss of class identity, except in terms of its income bracket. We therefore distinguish three income classes of equal size in both rural and urban areas, each comprising one-third of the area population. The three classes designated correspond to reasonably well-defined socio-economic groups, with the bottom income groups corresponding very plausibly to those below the poverty line, while the equal sizes of the groups, in population terms, gives the easiest possible weighting system among the groups.[8]

Broadly speaking, as indicated already in the previous chapter, in rural areas the bottom class comprise landless agricultural labourers and poor peasants; the middle group consist largely of the more viable peasant farmers and those agricultural labourers who have adequate and regular wage employment; the top group are the landlord class and those farmers with a significant marketable surplus. In urban areas the bottom class are largely underemployed, even unemployed, deriving such incomes as they can, largely from the informal sector; industrial workers, those in the lower white-collar occupations and small traders largely make up the middle group, while the larger traders, businessmen and top-salary people comprise the top group. Thus although no classification based either on income or on socio-economic characteristics can avoid 'grey' areas, in designating our income groups we have tried to give them internal unity through their wider socio-economic characteristics. Moreover, the bottom income classes in both areas can be identified with the poverty groups, whose basic needs are not met. As we discussed above, the estimation of a poverty line is a not uncontroversial matter, and our designation of one-third of both the rural and urban population as below subsistence broadly conforms to several of the major estimates, while also representing a reasonable compromise between the very low figures, such as Sukhatme's 15-25 per cent, and the estimates of over 50 per cent. The division of the rural and urban income distribution into thirds implies a rather higher estimate of the poverty line, in income terms, in urban than in rural areas, again consistent with our earlier discussion.

The distribution of incomes, both as it is generated in production and as it underlies expenditure patterns, is obviously crucial to the structure and working of our model. The compilation of these distributions involved a substantial data exercise which is described fully in Chapter 3 below.

Consumption Expenditure

The importance of the income distribution for expenditure, in particular for the hypothesis concerning the employment potential of income redistribution, is predicated on differences in consumption patterns across income classes. Consequently the choice of the form of the commodity expenditure functions may have important implications for the estimates and policy conclusions drawn from the model. Paukert, Skolka and Maton (1976, p. 166) neatly pose the nature of the choice:

> In the model, we wanted to obtain the solution by a single matrix inversion. In order to avoid adjustment problems, we also wanted the consumption functions to fulfil the additivity condition. And the shift in the consumption distribution had to lead to a change in the pattern of the total private consumption and the level of total private savings . . . Unfortunately, there is no type of consumption function that would fulfil all these three conditions simultaneously.

They, and most other authors in this area, give priority to the first two of their criteria, that the functions should be linear and should satisfy the adding-up property, coupling this with the view that the nature of the data, from household budget surveys, justifies the adoption of Engel curves relating consumption of each commodity to the level of

income, with prices assumed constant. This leads to the specification of
Engel functions which are either wholly or piecewise linear, with a
marginal propensity to consume which is either constant for all income
levels or constant for given income ranges (classes) while varying
between them. While we concur in the exclusion of prices, the assumption of a constant marginal propensity to consume is excessively restric-
tive relative to the hypothesis being explored, particularly with only
three income classes (in each area). The same consideration applies to
the other form commonly adopted, the double log, which implies a
constant elasticity across income levels or as income changes; this form,
moreover, fails to meet the adding-up condition.

Since we regard accurate representation of the income elasticity at
different income levels as more important in its contribution to the
significance of our results than the convenience in solution offered by
linearity or the neatness of a common functional form, we follow the
general suggestion of Brown and Deaton (1972, Part III.1) that the
simpler forms used for Engel curves may be regarded as 'convenient
approximations to different ranges of the full sigmoid curve', and they
instance the double-log, linear and log-reciprocal forms. Our approach
has therefore been to select the functional form which gives the best fit
for the Engel curve over the range of our observations, where the dominant criterion for best fit is the acceptability of the implied consumption elasticity at different income levels, in the light of the status of the
commodity in household budgets and estimates from other studies. The
forms which we use include the power function[9] and log-log-inverse, in
addition to the commoner forms.

This flexible, empirically based approach can achieve adding-up consistency only by accident. One consumption sector, 'other services', has
therefore been designated as a residual, expenditure there being
whatever sum is required to secure consistency with total expenditure;
we draw some reassurance on the acceptability of the overall procedures from the fact that the implied estimates for the residual sector,
rural and urban, have rarely been implausible.

The other important route through which we have tried to trace
consumption relations as closely as possible is through detailed disaggregation by commodity. In all we distinguish 63 commodities or
commodity groups in consumption and fit expenditure functions for
these for rural and urban areas separately.

The main data source on consumption patterns, with a detailed
commodity breakdown, is the set of surveys carried out annually by the
NSS, and, less frequently, by the NCAER. In combination these provide

the data on which the Engel functions were estimated and the distributors applied in establishing the base-period allocation of consumption expenditure by sector between the rural and urban areas, and within each area, among the three income classes.[10]

Production and Employment

The use of a Leontief-type input-output system to determine industry-wide outputs and employment has well-known advantages and limitations. Its characteristic feature is its detailed specification, through the interindustry flow table, of the use of inputs purchased from other production sectors and so of the total output requirements from all sectors implicit in any pattern of final demand. For a study such as ours, as more generally for planning at a sectoral level, this tracing of the direct plus indirect effects of final demand is an advantage which far outweighs the limitations of the system.

The assumption of fixed coefficients in production, typically applied to both factor and non-factor inputs, largely precludes attempts to analyse input substitution in response to changing relative prices or to technical progress, even including neutral technical progress. However, alternative treatments of production relations which give primacy to relative factor prices, notably the Cobb-Douglas and constant-elasticity-of-substitution production functions, present their own methodological problems. While the data requirements for the construction of an input-output table are very considerable, particularly for interindustry purchases, only a single set are necessary, which need not be replicated on either a time-series or a cross-section basis; with detailed sectoral disaggregation the data requirements tend in practice to be less formidable for an input-output system than for the estimation of production functions at the industry level.[11]

A considerable amount of work has been done in India on the compilation of input-output tables and a number of these are now available from different sources and for different years.[12] While this gave us confidence, we could not, with our limited resources, consider constructing our own table. On the other hand, none of the existing tables could serve our purpose without considerable modification. Firstly we required a table for our base year, 1967-8. While the year-to-year stability of the structure of interindustry transactions means that a table for a not too distant year is acceptable for many purposes, the context of our overall macro-model required that at least the final demand and value added quadrants relate to 1967-8. More seriously, in the level of sectoral disaggregation used, none of the tables met our purposes. We wanted to achieve sufficient disaggregation of the production sectors to trace the impact of changes in the incomes and expenditure of our income groups, and also to capture any differences in employment intensity. These objectives implied a significantly greater disaggregation of agriculture and services than in any of the available tables. We therefore commissioned an updated version of Saluja's tables (Saluja, 1968, 1972), with suitable modifications to the sectoral disaggregation.[13]

Our table is larger, but only marginally, than that prepared by the Government of India Planning Commission (1973) in connection with the Fifth Plan, with 77 sectors against their 66,[14] and is prepared at producer prices of 1967-8. The areas in which we have concentrated the additional disaggregation are agriculture, construction and services, sectors which are usually very large and rather heterogeneous. We have divided agriculture into 12 sectors, as against the Planning Commission's three, construction into four (Planning Commission one), and services into seven, two for transport and five others (Planning Commission two for transport and one other).

A further objective which we hoped to meet through commodity disaggregation was the differentiation of the formal and informal sectors. Commodity-based categories are a far from ideal basis for this as many commodities are produced in both sectors; but since the distinction is not used in the compilation of interindustry flows commodity disaggregation has to serve as the best approximation. For this reason our sectoral classification distinguishes cigarettes and cigars (a product of the organised sector) and other tobacco products (from the informal sector), sugar and gur, vanaspati and other oils, and pukka and other construction.

The assumption that labour requirements are proportional to gross output is a natural extension of the Leontief framework. We have chosen to adopt a simple 'head count' approach to employment, without differentiation by occupation, skill or other characteristic. Some degree of disaggregation along such lines would be possible within our framework, although the data problems would be severe; but there is little evidence in India of significant labour shortages at any particular skill or educational level, except at seasonal peaks in some areas, suggesting that this would not be a relevant constraint on the production side; and on the income distribution side we have already aimed to capture socio-economic characteristics, at least broadly, in our designation of the income classes.[15]

In any labour-surplus economy estimating employment levels

presents serious conceptual problems,[16] particularly in the subsistence sector and where activities are of a seasonal nature. Moreover, effective use of the data on employment which is available from various sources in India is hampered by differences in definitions and coverage. Because of limitations of coverage it was not possible to work with only a single source although, for reasons of consistency, we tried to confine ourselves to as few as possible.[17] The best overall sources, in terms of comprehensiveness and detail of coverage, were the two Population Censuses (1961 and 1971), and these were adopted for the non-agricultural sectors. In agriculture, however, the census tabulations present cultivators and agricultural labourers only as one group, with no differentiation by crop. For the agricultural sectors, therefore, the Farm Management Surveys (FMS) carried out by the Ministry of Agriculture were adopted as the main basis for the preparation of the estimates.

The principal difficulty in estimating employment in the agricultural sectors on the basis of the FMS was the conversion from man days of labour input in the survey areas to man years for the country as a whole. For each crop sector a weighted average of the figures on man days of labour input per hectare from the various surveys was prepared and applied to the total area under cultivation for the relevant crop in 1967-8. These estimates of total man days of employment per crop were then converted into man years, with 300 man days taken as the equivalent of the man year. Our estimates of agricultural employment, being reckoned as the full man year equivalents of recorded man days are therefore much lower than the majority of alternative estimates, which are typically based on a count of workers by their industry of principal employment.[18]

For our 66 non-agricultural sectors, plus three agricultural sectors for which adequate information was not available from the FMS, the employment levels in 1967-8 were derived by interpolation between the levels for 1961 and 1971 recorded in the Population Censuses.

Throughout our subsequent discussions of employment levels and the employment implications of alternative policies, it is important to keep in mind the basis of our employment figures. In agriculture our concept of a man year of employment is the relatively stringent one of 300 man days; this greatly reduces our employment total by comparison with alternative estimates. For many of the industrial sectors and the organised services sector, where the majority of employees will be in full-time employment, the census record of workers per sector may not be a significant overstatement. But, particularly in the informal services sector, where a full man day is difficult even to specify precisely, the census basis may imply some overestimate of employment relative to the other sectors.

Exogenous Elements

Apart from consumption the other constituents of final demand, investment, stock-building, government purchases, exports and imports are treated exogenously.

It is perhaps surprising to find imports among these. In many applications imports are divided into those which are 'complementary', treated as a necessary input and related to gross output through a fixed coefficient as with other inputs, and those which are 'competitive', alternatives to domestic output in final use. Our treatment makes them all competitive or, more accurately, exogenous. Import controls in India have often been severe and the promotion of import substitution a conscious objective of policy;[19] import volume varies widely with the state of the harvest. These various considerations suggest that imports are more appropriately treated on a discretionary basis outside the model than mechanically within it.

The other element of final demand which is not infrequently endogenised is investment, as in dynamic input-output models. This approach, however, accentuates the restrictiveness of the assumptions of the input-output model; investment requirements are based on a fixed capital/output ratio which assumes no pre-existing excess capacity, no factor substitution and only, at best, Harrod-neutral technical progress. Moreover, the relevant capital/output ratio is the marginal one and systematic use of the average to proxy this may be misleading in practice. In view of the rigidities implied in the dynamic input-output formulation, coupled with an extensive, although variable, degree of excess capacity in Indian industry, we decided that it was preferable in a simulation context to treat the matter of supply limitations and requirements for additional capacity and investment in a discretionary manner and outside the formal structure of the model.

Against capital requirements must be set the availability of savings. The total volume of savings, from personal, corporate and government sources, is generated endogenously within the model, and, in principle, the dynamic aspects of the model could be represented, in Harrod-Domar fashion, by imposing the necessary consistency of savings with endogenous or exogenous capital requirements. Again, we develop this aspect to only a limited degree and in a discretionary way outside the model. Savings are generated in very different sectors while capital requirements are also disparately located; only a perfect capital market could secure the necessary detailed matching of the one with the other. In a country like India, where the opportunities for ensuring the flow of savings between institutions and sectors are very limited, the total volume of savings generated can be, at best, only a very approximate consistency check against capital requirements.

Concluding Remarks

The structure of our model takes the relatively familiar semi-closed Leontief form but with non-linear expenditure functions. Certain elements, notably investment, imports and exports, which could be at least partially endogenised, are left exogenous. Moreover, the degree of articulation adopted in the treatment of employment is obviously less than is possible, both conceptually and empirically. In each case this is due primarily to the limited practical usefulness, for our purposes, of further extensions rather than to inadequacy of the data.

The most important innovatory feature is the application of the model to India, involving in particular the derivation of the distribution of incomes by income class and area from the pattern of production. We turn now to the key topic of the distribution of incomes.

Notes

1. For a good discussion of Leontief models see Taylor (1975).
2. ILO itself (ILO, 1971a), in a technical paper accompanying the report of an inter-agency team on employment strategy for Ceylon (Sri Lanka) gives a formal outline of an open Leontief model and a few estimates for a very aggregated version comprising two income classes and three production sectors (agriculture, industry and services). The more detailed work of Paukert, Skolka and Maton (1976), discussed below, was carried out later at the ILO. The impact of more rapid growth rates of income or consumption for poorer groups has been explored quite widely for Latin America, by Foxley (1976) for Chile, Tokman (1976) for Venezuela and Morley and Smith (1973) for Brazil, while Cline (1972) for Argentina, Brazil, Mexico and Venezuela concentrates particularly on the impact through savings. Morley and Williamson (1974) examine the employment implications of alternative growth paths using data for Brazil. The static effect of income distribution on income and employment levels is estimated by Paukert, Skolka and Maton (1976) for the Philippines, in a model with 10 income classes and 64 production sectors; they also extend the model to incorporate a consistency check between total savings generated and gross fixed investment. A very similar methodology, usually with rather less detail, is used by Soligo (1973) for Pakistan, Sunman (1973) for Turkey, and Ho (1976) and Chinn (1977), both for Taiwan, while for several countries of Latin America the employment potential for industry alone is estimated (Figueroa, 1975; Tokman, 1974). A more detailed survey, particularly of the earlier models, is given in Cline (1975).

3. A good discussion of closed Leontief models is given in Clark (1975). See also Manne (1974).

4. Since our work was completed the degree of closure in macro-models of income distribution has been significantly extended in the work of Adelman and Robinson (1978) and Rodgers, Hopkins and Wéry (1978). Adelman and Robinson present a 'computable general equilibrium model' for Korea which endogenises both factor and product prices through sets of supply-demand relationships; resource use is determined by neo-classical production functions, although intermediate purchases are treated in a fixed-coefficient manner; the distribution of household incomes is built up through factor payments. Rodgers, Hopkins and Wéry in their model of the Philippines introduce substantial disaggregation on the demographic side in determining labour supply and so wages, employment and household incomes. Both these models are highly non-linear.

5. Adelman and Robinson (1978) in their study of Korea for the World Bank incorporate some elements of this approach. Its appropriateness is also discussed in Pyatt and Roe (1977, especially p. 48) but they too are unable to implement it. See also Chenery and Duloy (1974).

6. For a full description see Chapter 3 below.

7. Some of these aspects have already been developed in Chapter 1.

8. Foxley (1976) and Tokman (1975), for example, distinguish only two groups in this way. Weisskoff (1976) on the other hand uses 15 classes. A common division is by deciles.

9. Zarembka (1972, 1974).

10. For details of the data used and the fitting of the expenditure functions, see Kadekodi and Pearson (1978).

11. An experimental attempt to construct and use a model with input-output coefficients for commodities but a CES production function for labour and capital inputs is described in Chenery and Raduchel (1971). See also Adelman and Robinson (1978).

12. The earliest exercises were carried out by the Indian Statistical Institute (ISI) in the 1950s; for a short history see Ghosh (1968). See also Saluja (1968, 1972), Government of India Planning Commission (1973), Mathur *et al.* (1968) and Venkatramaiah *et al.* (1972).

13. The input-output table was prepared by M.R. Saluja of the Indian Statistical Institute, Delhi. For further details see Saluja (1978).

14. In their model for 1978-83 the Planning Commission have now adopted an 89-sector classification with more disaggregation in agriculture and services.

15. For an interesting attempt to incorporate the occupational structure of employment in an input-output framework for India, at a much more aggregated level than ours, see Gaiha (1977). More generally see Chenery and Duloy (1974).

16. See particularly Sen (1975, Parts I-III).

17. The estimation of sector-wise employment was carried out by Dr M.S. Ramanujam, in collaboration with K. Raghavan, of the Institute of Applied Manpower Research, New Delhi. For details see Ramanujam and Raghavan (1978).

18. Three other estimates of agricultural employment were also prepared. For further details, see Ramanujam and Raghavan (1978, especially pp. 10-11 and 17).

19. See, for example, the Fifth Plan, Government of India Planning Commission (1973a).

3 THE DISTRIBUTION OF VALUE ADDED AMONG INCOME CLASSES

The levels of personal income in individual socio-economic groups are the predominant — and certainly, for all their difficulties, the most easily measured — determinants of their consumption levels and so, to a degree, of their standard of life. And although fiscal and inter-personal transfers may be very important for individual households, these income levels are essentially determined by the incomes earned in production. In this chapter we look in detail at these two aspects, firstly the size distribution of personal incomes across socio-economic groups, and secondly its origins in terms of the shares of the different groups in the value added created by the production sectors. The analysis will be conducted largely in terms of the two-stage concept of the generation of factor incomes and their translation into personal incomes by socio-economic group, outlined in Chapter 2. The production process, in utilising factor services, gives rise to payments to the owners or providers of these, as wages, crop income and rent of landowners, profits, dividends and interest payments to the owners of real or financial capital, and mixed income to the self-employed; according to the distribution of ownership of the factor services employed, the distribution of personal incomes across households is generated.

This is the first time to our knowledge that an analysis of this sort has been carried out for India, and formidable difficulties, conceptual and practical, were encountered both in measuring income and in defining its sources. These difficulties tend to be particularly acute for precisely those groups which are our main focus of interest, the lowest income classes in both rural and urban areas, who derive a very substantial part of their incomes in non-monetary form, or from the informal sector or, frequently, both. For the peasant proprietor the imputation of his income through household consumption of his farm produce presents well-known problems of measurement and valuation. In a labour-surplus economy the imputed value of family labour is often a major part of household income, but on measurement a consensus exists only that its opportunity cost is lower than its market price, but not how much lower; this problem applies equally to agricultural households and to small-scale industrial or trading enterprises run essentially on a family basis. Apart from the imputation aspect, these are also areas where information on the cash payments made is scanty. While measurement of the level of income is subject to substantial variation with the assumptions adopted in imputing values where cash flows are non-existent or inadequately recorded, its division between factors as wages, profits and rent, however appropriate and feasible in principle, is possible in practice only on the most arbitrary basis. For these various reasons, while we believe the exercise to be an extremely important one, we present our estimates essentially as a first attempt and not a definitive measurement of the distribution of income as it arises from value added in production.

Distribution of Personal Incomes: Previous Estimates

Before tracing its origins, however, we will first consider the distribution of personal incomes, an area which has for some years been the subject of considerable investigation in India. As in most developing countries, there exists no comprehensive set of data on household or personal income in India, although sample surveys, on a nationwide basis, are conducted at intervals by the National Council of Applied Economic Research (NCAER). Moreover, some studies have been made of the distribution of income, based on a combination of the National Sample Survey (NSS) data on the distribution of consumption expenditure between expenditure classes, the Central Statistical Organisation (CSO) national income accounts, income tax data, and figures for household savings from the Reserve Bank of India.

The NCAER has conducted a number of studies, at the household level, of the distribution of income and patterns of savings and expenditure (e.g. NCAER, 1962, 1964-5, 1965, 1966, 1972, 1975). These are the only available primary sources of data on personal incomes.[1]

All other available estimates of the distribution of incomes are derived by combining data from various sources. A leading example of this method is by Ojha and Bhatt (1974); starting from the CSO national income data they deduct estimated direct taxes paid by unincorporated enterprises and savings by households to obtain total consumption expenditure; this is then allocated across expenditure classes following the NSS expenditure distribution; the expenditure distribution is then transformed into a distribution of incomes by the assumption that all net saving is by the top expenditure class, with saving and dissaving by households exactly in balance within all other classes. The distribution derived by Ojha and Bhatt by this method as an average for 1963-4 and 1964-5 is remarkably similar to the distribution for 1964-5 obtained in the NCAER 1964-5 survey (Bardhan, 1974, p. 107).

Ahmed and Bhattacharya (1972) similarly base their estimated distribution on the NSS expenditure distribution but converted to an income basis by the incorporation of data from income tax assessments.[2]

As Bardhan's detailed critique points out (Bardhan, 1974) none of these sources is wholly reliable. The samples used by the NCAER in its surveys tend to be rather small; e.g. in 1964-5, 3,331 households for the whole of India. In addition, in that survey certain groups of the population were unrepresented, the non-household population, those in inaccessible regions and others amounting in total to almost 10 per cent of the national population. The CSO figures, which might be expected to be the obvious benchmark, are themselves open to doubt: 'the CSO national income estimates themselves are on quite shaky foundations, particularly in respect of unorganised industry, trade, services, etc. Thus one should not put too much faith on comparison with CSO estimates'[3] (p. 106). When the estimates of total personal income from the NCAER and CSO are compared, after adjustment for differences in coverage and concept, the discrepancy between them amounts to as much as 25 per cent of the CSO estimate (p. 106). The NSS survey data on consumption expenditure utilises a much bigger sample than the NCAER, but suffers from a similar problem of incomplete coverage. The NSS sampling frame excludes the homeless, which may distort the results, particularly for the urban sector. As in the case of NCAER estimates of income and consumption, the NSS provides lower estimates both for individual commodities and/or aggregate consumption expenditure than the CSO.[4] However, in view of the limitations of the national income estimates it may not be appropriate to judge the reliability of the NSS estimates on the basis of their consistency or otherwise with the CSO data.[5]

Even if the NSS figures are accepted as an adequate representation of the distribution of household expenditure, its conversion into a distribution of household incomes raises further problems. Total household savings have been estimated by the Reserve Bank of India (RBI), the CSO and the NCAER; each, however, adopts its own methodology, involving assumptions about allocation proportions and blowing-up ratios, and the results, not surprisingly, differ substantially. Moreover, even when total savings have been estimated, their allocation across income classes remains unresolved. The use of income tax data as a guide to incomes in the higher brackets is equally liable to frustration. Less than 1 per cent of the population pay income tax and the incidence of tax avoidance and evasions designed to blur the distinction between income and wealth will, by affecting the different income groups differently, tend to distort the distribution of incomes.

Thus, whichever source or method of estimation is adopted the estimated distribution of income will remain open to doubt. In the case of the present study the problem is particularly complicated as we seek not only an all-India distribution but distributions for rural and urban areas separately, and distributions which are also consistent with the evidence from the side of production, on the distribution of value added by type of factor income and class of recipient.

Present Estimates

For the present study we have used an alternative derivation of the distribution of personal incomes integrating information from the NSS, NCAER and CSO. Three major considerations determined the general approach. First, much the best distributional data available are contained in the NSS, but they relate to household expenditure with no information given on household income. Secondly, the appropriate basis for mapping from an expenditure distribution to an income distribution is through an explicit consumption-income relationship rather than through alternative fragmentary information; the only systematic cross-section data on the aggregate consumption-income relationship at the household level are in the NCAER surveys. Finally, while the CSO estimates of aggregate consumption and disposable income may not be totally reliable, the need for consistency within our overall macro-model with other elements taken from the national income accounts requires that the estimated distributions give totals or mean values consistent with CSO figures.

The derivation of the distributions of personal disposable incomes in rural and urban areas, synthesising data from these three sources, was achieved in the following way, by using an approach similar in some respects to that of Iyengar and Jain (1973). First the distribution of consumption expenditure *per capita* was established by fitting a log-normal distribution to the NSS data from the 22nd Round (1967-8), with rural and urban households treated separately.[6] The relationship between aggregate *per capita* consumption and *per capita* income, again for rural and urban areas separately, was derived from the NCAER data for 1967-8; the functional form was left as flexible as possible by fitting the general power function form, but when the estimates proved not significantly different from the familiar double-log form this latter was adopted. Intercept adjustments were later applied to these functions to ensure compatibility between average *per capita* consumption and average *per capita* disposable income as estimated by the CSO (the separate rural and urban estimates of consumption and disposable income were obtained by applying to the CSO all-India data the NSS rural-urban proportions for consumption and the NCAER proportions for income). With consumption lognormally distributed and loglinearly related to income, income itself takes a lognormal distribution with its parameters determined by these relationships.[7] The desired groupings, in our case three equal-sized classes in both rural and urban areas, are then imposed on it.

Some of the principal values for *per capita* income, expenditure and savings implied by the income and expenditure distributions are shown in Table 3.1, page 72. Many of these are quite striking. The average level of *per capita* disposable income is 49 per cent higher in urban than in rural areas. For the lowest income groups the urban/rural differential is distinctly lower (37 per cent) than the average, and increases with income to a differential of 53 per cent in the top groups. In the case of *per capita* expenditure, the urban/rural differentials are lower, 38 per cent on the average, 48 per cent in the top group but only 18 per cent in the bottom group.

A more accurate comparison of real income and expenditure levels between rural and urban areas requires adjustment for price differences. As discussed earlier, prices in urban areas are probably between 8 and 15 per cent higher than in rural areas, and on the upper estimate rising from 11-12 per cent on the consumption basket of the poorest groups to nearly 20 per cent for the top income groups (Chatterjee and Bhattacharya, 1974, p. 195). Correction for price differences would thus reduce, but by no means eliminate, the urban advantage in incomes and expenditure. On the other hand rural incomes and expenditure may be somewhat overstated relative to their urban levels since the NSS values cash purchases at local prices but consumption of home-grown products at peak harvest prices.

One of the simplest ways of comparing our estimates with those of others, is to use one of the standard measures of inequality, the Gini coefficient. In our estimate the Gini coefficient of the distribution of income is 0.41 for rural areas and 0.44 for urban, figures which are approximately consistent with other estimates. The only data from which direct estimates can be made are from the NCAER. Using this source Bhatty (1974) estimates the Gini coefficient for rural areas to be 0.46 for 1967-8, somewhat higher than our estimate. However, for other years estimates based on the NCAER data vary between 0.35 and 0.41. The lowest estimate, 0.32, is by Ojha and Bhatt (1974) for the period 1963-4 and 1964-5. Allowing for the year-to-year fluctuation in the concentration ratio in the rural areas,[8] attributable partly to agricultural fluctuations and partly to the variability associated with small samples, our rural estimates fall within the range indicated by the NCAER data. For the urban areas our estimate is much the same as the estimates of NCAER and Ojha and Bhatt.

One point of difference should, however, be mentioned. Our estimates, like those of Ojha and Bhatt, indicate that incomes are slightly more equally distributed in rural than in urban areas,[9] while according to the NCAER sources there is no significant difference. The NSS consumption distribution, on which our consumption distribution is based, also suggests that consumption is more evenly distributed in rural areas than in the urban.

On our estimates consumption expenditure, which is a more relevant measure of the level of living, is more equally distributed, in both rural and urban areas, than incomes. Studies on more disaggregated levels have come to a similar conclusion. For instance Bhatty (1974, pp. 303-4) suggests that the inequality in the distribution of *per capita* consumption expenditure is uniformly less than the inequality of incomes in all states and among all the three categories of rural population (i.e. cultivators, agricultural workers and non-agricultural workers).

Both this result, and its source in savings behaviour, are familiar from many other countries. Table 3.1 clearly brings out the role of savings. According to our estimates the poorest two-thirds of the population both in rural and urban areas have negative saving; only the upper third saves. In a country like India where poor people have to borrow even for their day-to-day consumption expenses, dissaving by such people is not surprising. What may be questionable is the magnitude of the dissaving. On our estimates the poorest 33 per cent of the rural population had a *per capita* dissaving of Rs 77 against their total consumption expenditure of Rs 171. However, our finding in this respect is replicated in a number of other investigations using different data and methods.[10]

Distribution of Value Added among Income Classes

Once we had established the distribution of personal incomes in both rural and urban areas, and identified the income levels which mark the bounds between the various classes, the major task confronting us was the allocation of value added from each of the 77 production sectors into the six designated classes of personal income, three rural and three urban, plus 'other incomes' of the corporate and government sectors. No data source provides anything approaching comprehensive information on this, and it was beyond the scope of the study to undertake new data collection. We have therefore had to proceed on a piecemeal basis, devising a variety of methods to take advantage of such data as are available. The main objective of our method has been, as far as data permits, to break down value added in each sector into its constituent categories of factor income, identified by the institutional status of the recipient, and, through information on their size distribution, allocate the incomes received among the appropriate classes.

This method involves two major limitations, in addition to those imposed by the inadequacies of the data. It presupposes that incomes produced correspond exactly to incomes received, apart from the incidence of income taxes which we deduct but which are relatively unimportant in India, affecting only the very top income levels. Transfers between households, which are impossible to trace, are assumed to take place only within and not between groups, or, if between groups, then only in exactly offsetting amounts, such that all net flows are zero. To the extent that these assumptions are inaccurate the distribution of incomes received, as between income classes and between rural and urban areas, will be distorted. The second major limitation stems from the fact that factor incomes are paid to individuals while levels of *per capita* income and consumption are determined by household income. Information traced from the side of incomes paid out cannot distinguish where these are the sole, principal, or subsidiary incomes for the recipient household. In a country like India where, particularly among poorer groups, even the head of the household may derive his income piecemeal from more than one sector and several members may make significant contributions to household income, this method is liable to classify some small incomes inappropriately to the bottom class. On the other hand, where the size distribution of earnings by sector is traced from the side of the sources of household income, classification of the household on the basis of the occupation and income of its head is again liable to cause distortions. This problem — which applies in principle and, to some extent, in practice to economies at all levels of development — is essentially intractable without either the cross-classification of income earners by household status or the detailing of household incomes by all sources.[11]

In spite of the limitations of method and data, however, the insights which are gained into the sources of the distribution of incomes and the implications which sectoral growth patterns may have for it seem more than sufficient to validate the exercise.

Table 3.1: Patterns of Disposable Income, Expenditure and Savings, 1967-8

Population groups*	per capita income ranges (in Rs)	Share in income (%)	Average per capita disposable income (Rs)	per capita expenditure ranges (in Rs)	Share in average expenditure (%)	Average per capita expenditure (Rs)	Average per capita savings (Rs)
Rural							
Bottom	Less than 266	11	171	Less than 322	17	248	-77
Middle	Between 266 and 522	26	376	Between 322 and 509	30	427	-51
Top	Over 522	63	942	Over 509	53	780	162
All classes		100	495		100	485	11
Gini coefficient		0.41			0.29		
Urban							
Bottom	Less than 373	10	234	Less than 401	15	293	-59
Middle	Between 373 and 764	25	540	Between 401 and 692	28	557	-17
Top	Over 764	65	1443	Over 692	57	1153	290
All classes		100	737		100	668	70
Gini coefficient		0.44			0.34		

* The groups both in the rural and urban areas consist of bottom 33%, middle 34% and top 33%; 80.8% of the population is rural and 19.2% is urban.

Source: own estimates.

Agriculture: Crop Income

The agricultural sectors, taken together, provide by far the largest
source of incomes and employment in India, and substantial amounts
of information are available on many aspects of Indian agriculture.
Very little of this, however, relates directly to the cropwise sources of
income and their size distribution. Partly because of the extensive but
somewhat unsystematic nature of the data available, and partly because
of its deficiencies, the method eventually adopted for allocating the
value added of the agricultural sectors among the income classes proved
complex and laborious.[12] Two categories are distinguished for personal
incomes derived from crop production: crop income, received by farm
owners and cultivators; and wage income, received by hired labour. In
each sector these two categories are distributed separately across
income classes and then aggregated to give the class share in the sector's
value added.

The only primary source of data on incomes received by cultivators
which gives the necessary degree of disaggregation are the various Farm
Management Surveys (FMS) conducted between 1967 and 1971.[13]
These reports, some 20 in all, each for a different state or, less frequently, for a different year in one state, give very detailed information,
in total and by crop, on input use, costs of production and output
levels.

In the case of crop income, income produced and income received
are identical, making this part of the distributional relationship particularly straightforward. However, the FMS group cultivators by farm size
whereas we designate classes on an income basis. The link between disposable income received and crop income produced could not, therefore, be the direct one, but had to be established through a relationship
between each of these and farm size. With the level of *per capita*
income related to farm size, our income class bounds could be converted into farm size bounds. A further relationship, for any crop, between
farm size and crop income produced allowed the conversion of the
farm size bounds into crop income levels and so the calculation of class
shares in crop income.

In estimating the distribution of crop income across income classes
from any crop (sector) the first step was to establish average disposable
income *per capita*, for each farm size group, by deducting from the
value of gross output all costs, including wages paid to hired
labour.[14] *Per capita* income was then to be related to farm size by
regression, using the group means as observations. In our first attempt
we sought to make maximum use of the information available by fitting

this relationship for each state survey separately; the income class bounds could then be converted into farm size bounds which would be specific to each state, thus reflecting the variation between states in land quality and other relevant influences. This method, however, proved to be overdemanding of the data. The FMS employ only a small number of farm size groups, typically five, giving at best two observations in each income group.[15] In a number of cases, moreover, the observations were poorly spread; for Assam, for example, they all fell into the bottom class, while in the Punjab and Uttar Pradesh they all fell into the top class. As a result a number of the farm size bounds fitted on a statewise basis were unacceptable (in the most extreme cases actually negative) or, even where the bounds appeared not unacceptable, the resulting distribution of crop income proved implausible.

With some reluctance, therefore, we pooled the observations from all the available statewise surveys to establish an overall relationship between farm size and disposable income.[16] In spite of the apparently dubious implicit assumption that one hectare of cultivated land has equivalent income generating properties wherever located, this overall relationship fitted reasonably well and farm size bounds corresponding to the income class bounds were established.[17] Cultivators were thus allocated among the income classes on the basis of the size of their farms.

The distribution of farm sizes varies across states as well as across crops. The next step in the method was therefore to establish, for any crop, the relationship in any survey state between farm size and crop income received. This was again done by regression on group means. Superimposing the farm size bounds then gave the allocation of crop income among the farm size/income classes. For each crop therefore we derived a set of class shares in crop income, one distribution for each state for which a survey had been conducted.

The final problem was the derivation, for each crop, of an all-India distribution from the various distributions for individual states (with wage income added as discussed below). The country was subdivided into zones, each zone characterised as broadly homogeneous, for each crop. Typically, around six zones were used, and states for which no survey information was available were zoned along with survey states with similar geographical and ecological features. Where a zone included more than one survey state their distributions were averaged using their respective areas under the crop as weights. The distributions for the various zones were in turn aggregated, again weighted by area under the crop.

In this way the distribution of crop income from each sector among the income classes was built up from relationships between disposable income and farm size on the one hand and between farm size and crop income on the other, the latter relationship incorporating substantial amounts of distributional information, both state specific and crop specific.

Agricultural Wage Income

Although typically a smaller component of income than crop income, the allocation of agricultural wages among the income classes presented us with a more intractable problem. The FMS identify only wages paid out and offer no information about the income or other status of the recipients. The result was that the conversion of wages paid out into a distribution of wage incomes received, by crop, by states or even in total, could be achieved from FMS data only on the basis of quite arbitrary assumptions. Moreover, since they are surveys of cultivators, the ·FMS do not include landless labourers, who receive a substantial part of agricultural wage incomes.

The NCAER (1975), however, reports on incomes received by rural households, classified by source of income and farm size; by making use of this information we were able to allocate agricultural wages paid out among our recipient income classes. As with crop income, the method adopted involved the linking of wages received to disposable income through farm size, although differences in the format of the data resulted in some alterations in the method.

First, farm size (in terms of gross cropped area) was related by regression to *per capita* disposable income, and bounds on farm size were then derived to correspond to the income class bounds on disposable income.[18] Agricultural wages received per household were then regressed on farm size, using NCAER data consisting of group averages (in this set of data, farm size was classified only in terms of gross cropped area and not in terms of land ownership). The share of each income group in agricultural wages was estimated by integration of the areas described by the curve relating wages and farm size, and by the bounds on farm size. Finally, since agricultural wage income received was classified on a per household basis, the resulting shares had to be adjusted to a *per capita* basis by weighting each group's share by the inverse of the ratio of its average household size to the overall mean household size.[19]

The major limitation of this method is that it yields only a single distribution of wages across income classes; this distribution is then

applied across all crops and all states. The limited nature of the data
makes this inevitable, since the NCAER presents its data only on an
all-India all-crop basis. It can also be argued that distinguishing the
wages of hired agricultural labour by crop of origin will not, on occa-
sion, be particularly meaningful. But crop income is the more important income component and its distribution varies both by crop and by
state, as do the relative shares of wages and crop income in value added
(the distribution of wage income is added to the distribution of crop
income at the state/crop level, before any aggregation). With these
other sources of distributional variation captured, the limitation
implied by the single all-crop distribution of wages will, it is hoped, not
be too significant.

While agricultural activities are predominantly rural, some income is
derived from agriculture in urban areas. The national income accounts
are of little help here. Consequently, we decided to build up an estimate on the basis of average incomes received and shares in the agricultural population. The NCAER in its Rural Income Survey (1975)
gives information on *per capita* crop income and agricultural wages
received in rural households. We assumed these averages to apply in
urban areas also.[20] The numbers of cultivators and agricultural wage
earners (a distinction which cannot be made with any precision) are
given, for rural and urban areas separately, in the Population Census.
The shares of the rural and urban areas in total value added in agriculture were then derived as weighted averages of the incomes of cultivators and wage earners in the two areas, where the weights were the
numbers in each group in the respective areas. The resulting distribution, 98 per cent to rural income classes and 2 per cent to urban,[21] was
applied to all agricultural sectors. The distribution across income classes
derived for the rural areas was applied to incomes from the agricultural
sectors in urban areas also.

Animal husbandry is a troublesome sector for the analysis of sources
and distribution of income. Since it is usually practised only as a part,
and typically a subsidiary part, of wider agricultural activities, identification of the income and costs attributable to it is difficult. Moreover,
livestock are largely fed on agricultural residues and kitchen waste, and
if purchase costs for feed and fodder required are imputed along with
the market value of output then net product is often negative.[22] We
did undertake the detailed allocation of the sector's value added
between rural and urban areas. Surveys by the Institute of Agricultural
Research Statistics (IARS) gave the rural-urban location of cow and
buffalo milk production, which were aggregated and weighted by value

added per kg of each type of milk,[23] to give the rural-urban distribution of income from milk. Value added from meat products and animal by-products was divided in proportion to the estimated animal populations of the two areas,[24] while fishing was assumed to be a rural activity. The outcome of this exercise was a distribution of value added from animal husbandry virtually identical to the 98 per cent rural, 2 per cent urban division which we had derived for crop production. From the detailed scrutiny of available data sources for this sector we concluded that no adequate basis existed for the allocation of incomes received across the income classes. This distribution along with that for other agriculture, for which cropwise information was very incomplete, was therefore derived as a residual, the shares of each group being determined by iteration between plausibility and the required level of *per capita* income, from all sectors, in each class.

Non-Agricultural Sectors

For the non-agricultural sectors our general objective was to subdivide sectoral value added as far as possible into detailed categories of factor income and build up the distribution by socio-economic group through these. The various categories of factor income which we aimed to identify are shown in Figure 3.1, page 79.

In each sector the categories of factor income[25] were then aggregated into 'other incomes' (retentions, including corporate tax) and three categories of personal income: wages (including the mixed incomes of the unorganised sector which could not be subdivided by factor category); salaries; and 'distributions'.

Manufacturing Sectors

The manufacturing sectors, and we distinguish 47 of them, together create approximately 14 per cent of national income and 17 per cent of employment in India. The major part of the incomes derived from manufacturing flows to urban areas and in establishing the distribution of incomes across the income classes we concentrate particularly on the urban groups. We begin by discussing the allocation of sectoral income between rural and urban areas.

The rural-urban distribution of income from the manufacturing sectors could not be traced on the basis of incomes received, but had to be proxied by the location of incomes produced. This will be an accurate representation in the case of the household sector, and inaccurate for the organised sector only to the extent that systematic net commuting or net income transfers occur between the areas.[26] The

CSO, in its disaggregated national accounts series (Government of India CSO, 1967, 1975), distinguishes value added for 20 industries in the registered sector, and seven more-aggregated groups in the unregistered sector.[27] We assumed that registered establishments would be located in urban areas only, while unregistered establishments could be located in either. The unregistered sector includes household and non-household small-scale establishments. For the household sector the NSS Surveys of Small-Scale Manufacture[28] can be used to derive the rural-urban distribution of value added. For lack of other information we assumed this distribution to apply also to the non-household part of the unregistered sector, and so to the unregistered sector as a whole. The availability of the rural-urban distribution of value added for the unregistered sector at the level only of seven industry groups was a significant limitation, as even with our assumption that the entire value added of the registered sector went to urban areas, the full rural-urban distribution could be derived only for these seven groups. We then assumed that the distribution for the aggregate group applied to each sector within it, including sectors where our disaggregation was more detailed than the CSO's 20 sectors.

The alternative to this method was to adopt the rural-urban distribution of the industry workforce as recorded in the Census of Population, combined with some assumption about the relative levels of value added per worker in the two areas, which would have to be based on virtually no information. The choice was thus between lack of sectoral detail but within known aggregates and guesstimation of some of the important parameters in the process of income generation. For the most part we preferred the former course, although in a small number of sectors the distribution was based on the working force.

The distribution of personal incomes across income classes in urban areas was carried out separately for the three major categories, wages, salaries and 'distributions'. For wages and salaries the method was similar but based on different data sources. For wages the Family Budget Surveys of Industrial Workers carried out by the Ministry of Labour report the distributions of income levels of wage earners, by income class, and the Middle Class Family Living Surveys conducted by the CSO similarly record the distribution of incomes among salary earners.[29] These surveys relate to 1958-9, and we assumed that the pattern of income distribution recorded then remained relevant for 1967-8.[30]

However, the data from these surveys represented wage levels and living standards for wage earners and middle class households in selected industrial centres, while we sought the distribution of incomes received

from individual industries. For each centre, therefore, for wage earners
and salary earners separately, the distribution of incomes was fitted
(proportion of households against average income *per capita*, by
income group) and income bounds for our three income classes imposed.
Since the distributions were extremely smooth, fitting by eye to a
graphical plot was entirely adequate. Thus the income shares received
by the households of wage and salary earners respectively who fell into
each of our three income classes were derived for each industrial centre
included in the surveys.

Figure 3.1: Flows of Sectoral Value Added

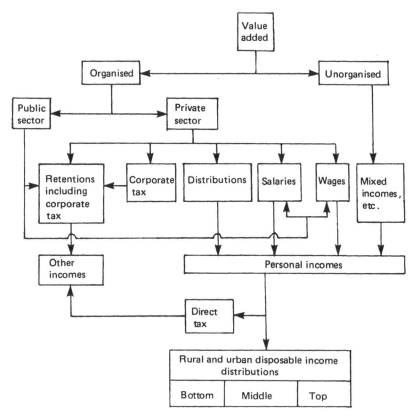

The citywise distributions were combined to form industry distributions through a detailed weighting procedure. Each survey reported the number of workers covered, by industry of employment; these were totalled by industry, and each centre given a weight corresponding to its share in the all-survey employment in that industry. The citywise distributions, for wages and salaries separately, were then aggregated using these weights.[31] Finally, the separate, now all-India, distributions of wages and salaries were aggregated within each industry, with all 'distributions' (distributed profits, interest and rent) allocated to the top class.

The employment provided by the manufacturing sector in rural areas is fairly small and systematic data on which to base a sectorwise distribution of incomes across classes virtually non-existent. From the NCAER Rural Income Survey (1975), we were able to derive two distributions, one for non-agricultural wages and one for salaries, across our income classes. For those industries judged to be small-scale the wage distribution alone was applied, and in those less exclusively small-scale, the weighted distribution of wages and salaries was applied.

Other Sectors

Workers in mining and plantations, as industrial sectors, were covered in the Family Budget Surveys discussed under manufacturing and the same method adopted. In these cases, however, part of the employment was located in surrounding villages rather than in the industrial centre and the survey correspondingly extended to include rural households. The income distributions for these sectors were therefore applied to both urban and rural areas. The overall distribution of sectoral value added between urban and rural areas was based on Population Census figures for the working population.

Construction is a large and heterogeneous industry where output, incomes and employment are poorly measured. The Population Census indicated the overall distribution of the workforce between rural and urban areas; we made the common-sense assumption that all value added generated in rural housing construction remained in the rural areas and derived the rural-urban shares for urban housing construction as a residual, on the grounds that much of this, particularly in smaller towns, is handled by small contractors whose workforce may be part-time in construction during slack agricultural periods. In its survey of income expenditure patterns, by class, across occupations, the NSS (19th Round) does not classify construction workers specifically; however, in view of the other categories listed we concluded that construction workers must be a substantial proportion of 'other occupations' in both rural and urban areas and adopted these distributions.

On incomes received from the various service sectors we had a mixture of very detailed information and total absence of information. For those services which we distinguish individually, education, medical services, entertainment, domestic service, the CSO provides a rural-urban breakdown of value added,[32] while the NSS (19th Round) Survey in its survey of expenditure levels by occupation gives good coverage of the professions and white-collar groups from which urban and rural distributions for the sectors were derived. Within 'other services' we had some information on trade and catering, business services and real estate which could be used to give guidelines, but partly for lack of comprehensive data and partly because overall consistency had to be achieved with total *per capita* income, from all sectors, for each of the six income classes, this sizeable sector was treated essentially as a residual.

Shares of Income Classes

The distribution of value added by sector between rural and urban areas and across income classes is shown, for broad industry groups, in Table 3.2, page 83, and for the full 77 sectors in Table 3.4, pages 87-8.

Looking first at the relative positions of the rural and urban areas, it is evident that the rural areas, containing 81 per cent of the population, receive by far the greater share in value added in primary activities, 97 per cent, but only 32 per cent of value added in manufacturing, and 51 per cent from services. Thus primary industries are heavily oriented towards the creation of income in rural areas, while manufacturing and services are urban biased. Within manufacturing, industries fall into two broad groups: those producing simpler, more labour-intensive products, food, leather and wood products, yield a much higher share for the rural areas than the so-called 'basic', capital-intensive industries, metals, engineering and chemicals, where the urban bias is particularly pronounced; the textile industries are an intermediate category, being fairly evenly divided between factory (urban) and cottage sectors.[33] When this distribution of personal incomes is extended to incorporate other incomes, received by companies and government, the share of value added going to the urban areas is even larger.

In the distribution across classes the most striking feature, almost inevitably, is the very small share received by the lowest income classes. There is not a single industry group, in either rural or urban areas, which does not yield a lower volume of income to the poorest third of the population than to the middle third; in this sense there is not a single industry group where the distribution of income favours the poor. In agriculture, however, which is the dominant source of income in the rural areas, particularly for the poor, the share received by the middle group is only marginally greater than the share of the bottom group. In part this reflects the greater importance of non-agricultural incomes for the middle income group, but it also tends to suggest that the major divide in agriculture may be between the rich and the others rather than between the poor and the others.

In rural areas the income position of the poorest class is dominated by agriculture; in both absolute and relative terms it is their leading source of income. Their share in agricultural incomes, 12 per cent, substantially exceeds their 7 per cent share in incomes from services, while they gain less than 4 per cent of incomes produced in industry. Although manufacturing industries are only minor sources of income in rural areas, a pattern is clear: for both the bottom and middle groups their income share is substantially greater in the light or consumer industries than in the basic industries. The income share of the rural middle class is particularly high in mining and plantations, services and animal husbandry. The miner is clearly a member of the wage-earning elite, while agricultural middlemen and traders also typically have regular and above-minimum incomes. The peasant who has sufficient capital to engage in animal husbandry and the stockman, again with year-round employment, are also likely to have middle-group status, although little emphasis should be placed on the interpretations of the income shares from animal husbandry, as they have been derived as a residual. In several industries the middle groups actually receive a larger share in income generated than the top group, reflecting their position as predominantly household industries with the household's wage plus profit income placing it in the middle group. By far the most skewed distribution of all, in terms of the share it gives to the top class, is for agriculture; the share going to the upper income groups, 73 per cent of agricultural incomes generated in rural areas, greatly exceeds their 44 per cent share in rural incomes from manufacturing and their 40 per cent share in service income.

On the urban side the dominance of agriculture is replaced by a greatly enhanced role for industry and services. The predominantly urban location of much of modern industry alongside substantial amounts of unregistered manufacturing, smooths out the share of the poorest group between industries. The position of the middle group, however, still shows some significant variation; it is particularly strong

Table 3.2 Estimated Distribution of Value Added by Industrial Sector Groups and by Rural/Urban Area, 1967-8 (in percentages)

Sector groups	Income groups Rural			
	Bottom	Middle	Top	Total
1. Agriculture	11.95	14.09	71.96	98.00
2. Animal husbandry	3.23	30.28	64.49	98.00
3. Total agriculture	10.87	16.10	71.03	98.00
4. Mining, plantations, etc.	6.66	30.50	42.36	79.58
5. Total primary (3 + 4)	10.68	16.77	69.71	97.16
6. Food products	7.15	27.98	23.69	58.82
7. Textiles	3.02	12.07	11.47	26.56
8. Wood products	5.91	23.42	20.22	49.55
9. Leather products	4.02	16.72	23.03	43.77
10. Chemicals, etc.	0.26	1.18	2.85	4.29
11. Metals and engineering	0.79	3.40	5.91	10.10
12. Other manufacturing	0.77	3.55	8.53	12.85
13. Total manufacturing	3.67	14.58	14.14	32.39
14. Services excluding other services	4.58	16.37	24.71	45.66
15. Total services	7.37	22.79	20.36	50.52
16. Total value added	8.64	18.58	45.49	72.71

Sector groups	Income groups Urban				Total (rural + urban)
	Bottom	Middle	Top	Total	
1. Agriculture	0.24	0.27	1.49	2.00	100
2. Animal husbandry	0.07	0.47	1.46	2.00	100
3. Total agriculture	0.22	0.29	1.48	2.00	100
4. Mining, plantations, etc.	6.83	7.14	6.44	20.42	100
5. Total primary (3+4)	0.53	0.61	1.71	2.84	100
6. Food products	4.44	8.27	28.48	41.18	100
7. Textiles, etc.	6.43	15.57	51.44	73.44	100
8. Wood products	4.75	14.10	31.61	50.45	100
9. Leather products	6.68	13.65	35.90	56.23	100
10. Chemicals, etc.	5.81	13.40	76.49	95.71	100
11. Metals and engineering	5.09	18.35	66.46	89.90	100
12. Other manufacturing	7.38	15.78	63.99	87.15	100
13. Total manufacturing	5.36	13.83	48.42	67.61	100
14. Services excluding other services	8.12	15.80	30.42	54.34	100
15. Total services	5.35	12.33	31.79	49.48	100
16. Total value added	2.82	6.36	18.11	27.29	100

in several of the manufacturing sectors, most notably metals and engineering, and in some services, reflecting the position of the industrial wage earner in regular employment and the lower white-collar worker. Interestingly, the share of the top group in income from manufacturing in urban areas almost exactly matches the top group share from agriculture in rural areas, at 72 per cent. This share does not vary greatly from industry to industry, although it is particularly high in chemicals and relatively low in wood and leather products. Their share in services, 64 per cent, implies a considerably more biased distribution than in rural areas where they receive only 40 per cent, but these figures were derived partly as residuals and must therefore be treated with caution.

The principal feature of our distributional exercise is its degree of detail, distinguishing 77 individual sectors in rural and urban areas separately. No other estimates of comparable scope exist with which detailed comparisons can be made. Some alternative estimates are, however, available for some of the major proportions in the distribution. An earlier study of the rural-urban distribution by Chakravarty and others (1960) distinguished 15 major sectoral groups. Since their estimates relate to 1952-3, the changing structure of the Indian economy and changes in relative prices over the intervening years, in addition to classification differences, make a strict comparison between their estimates and ours inappropriate. Nevertheless, the similarities between the two sets of estimates are striking. We estimate the rural share in income from agriculture, including animal husbandry, at 98 per cent against 97 per cent by Chakravarty. In mining our estimate of the rural share is 80 per cent, against 89 per cent, a difference which may reflect the increase in industrialisation over the 1950s and 1960s, with small mining centres developing into towns. Their estimate of a 59 per cent rural share in small-scale industry can be compared with our estimate of around 50 per cent for food, wood and leather products and textiles, all taken together, and their 47 per cent rural share for factory establishments with our 32 per cent for all manufacturing. Here again, increased urbanisation is to be expected with industrial development, and our classification is predominantly by sector and only indirectly by large and small scale. In transport, where a rural-urban allocation is difficult even in principle for considerable parts of value added, our estimate of one-third rural is close to their 35-39 per cent; the more realistic assessment may well be that both sets of estimates must be subject to significant margins of error. The only sizeable difference between the two sets of estimates is in the case of total services, where we estimate 46 per cent against 37 per cent. Part of this will be explicable in terms of the expansion in rural areas of Community Development Projects and the *Panchayat Raj*, although part may be residual error. The overall shares in total value added, where we estimate 73 per cent as against 70 per cent, are obviously remarkably close.[34]

Income Sources for the Poorest Groups

Since a particular focus of interest in our work is the position of the poorest groups whose basic needs are not being met, it is instructive to give more detailed consideration to the sources and structure of the incomes they receive.

Table 3.3, page 86, shows the relative importance of the various sectors as sources of income for the rural and urban poor respectively. For the rural poor agriculture provides no less than 63 per cent of their income, while services contribute a further 30 per cent. The manufacturing sectors together contribute only just over 5 per cent, and mining, plantations and forestry a further 2 per cent. By contrast, in urban areas manufacturing provides almost one-quarter of the incomes of the poorest group, with agriculture, along with mining and plantations, contributing a further 10 per cent. Comparable to agriculture's role for the rural poor is services, which provide virtually two-thirds of the income of the urban poor. Much of this derives from what may be broadly termed the 'informal' service sector.

It therefore appears that, from the point of view of policies aimed at improving the position of the poorest groups, two general conclusions emerge from our detailed analysis of income sources and income shares. The rural poor are heavily dependent on agriculture, and the urban poor on the informal service sector. In the longer run, if the process of development is to alleviate poverty, it must lift the poor out of this position into more productive and remunerative employment elsewhere. In the shorter run, a significant contribution to the alleviation of poverty, other than, or even in addition to, consumption transfers can be achieved only by giving these groups a considerably greater share in value added generated, particularly in these two dominant sectors.

Table 3.3: Sources of Income of Lowest Income Groups in Rural and Urban Areas, 1967-8 (in percentages)

Sector groups	Income groups	
	Rural	Urban
1. Agriculture (excluding animal husbandry)	60.73	3.81
2. Animal husbandry	2.32	0.15
3. Total agriculture	63.05	3.95
4. Mining, forestry and plantations	1.87	5.89
5. Total primary (3 + 4)	64.93	9.85
6. Food products manufacturing	3.24	6.15
7. Textiles and footwear manufacturing	0.76	5.00
8. Wood products, etc.	0.90	2.20
9. Leather and products	0.07	0.36
10. Chemicals and petroleum	0.02	1.07
11. Basic metals	0.31	6.10
12. Other manufacturing	0.11	3.32
13. Total manufacturing	5.40	24.20
14. Services (excluding other services)	6.35	34.52
15. Other services	23.32	31.42
16. Total services	29.67	65.95
17. Grand total (all sectors)	100.00	100.00

Table 3.4: Percentage Distribution of Value Added across Income Groups and Other Income, 1967-8

Sector	Rural Bottom	Rural Middle	Rural Top	Urban Bottom	Urban Middle	Urban Top	Other income	Sector share in total value added
1. Rice	26.8	18.6	52.6	0.5	0.4	1.1	0.0	11.4
2. Wheat	6.0	7.8	84.2	0.1	0.2	1.7	0.0	3.7
3. Pulses and Gram	6.3	4.7	87.0	0.1	0.1	1.8	0.0	3.0
4. Other foodgrains	6.0	7.8	84.2	0.1	0.2	1.7	0.0	5.4
5. Fruits, nuts, vegetables	5.8	8.3	83.9	0.1	0.2	1.7	0.0	6.4
6. Cotton	5.8	8.3	83.9	0.1	0.2	1.7	0.0	1.4
7. Jute	31.2	35.8	31.0	0.6	0.7	0.6	0.0	0.5
8. Oilseeds	13.5	7.6	76.9	0.3	0.2	1.6	0.0	2.7
9. Sugarcane	5.8	8.3	83.9	0.1	0.2	1.7	0.0	1.5
10. Tobacco	5.8	8.3	83.9	0.1	0.2	1.7	0.0	0.3
11. Other agriculture	3.2	30.3	64.5	0.1	0.5	1.5	0.0	6.0
12. Animal husbandry	3.2	30.3	64.5	0.1	0.5	1.5	0.0	6.0
13. Plantations	11.0	43.1	30.8	0.4	1.5	9.4	3.8	0.4
14. Tea and coffee	1.0	2.2	25.7	2.4	5.3	62.4	1.1	0.3
15. Forestry products	4.3	19.7	47.5	0.6	2.6	6.3	19.0	1.2
16. Coal	5.4	27.6	27.0	14.2	12.1	3.3	10.4	0.6
17. Miscellaneous coal products	0.7	3.0	7.2	7.7	16.6	55.8	9.0	0.0
18. Iron ore	5.4	27.7	27.1	14.2	12.2	3.3	10.1	0.1
19. Crude oil	4.3	21.9	21.4	11.3	9.6	2.6	28.9	0.2
20. Other minerals	5.2	26.7	26.1	13.7	11.7	3.2	13.4	0.2
21. Sugar	3.4	15.8	38.1	2.1	5.5	18.9	16.1	0.2
22. Gur	11.9	46.4	33.0	1.1	4.4	3.2	0.0	0.9
23. Vanaspati	0.7	3.4	8.3	3.6	7.9	70.0	6.1	0.0
24. Vegetable oils	9.3	36.4	26.0	1.9	3.9	18.5	4.1	0.8
25. Cigarettes and cigars	1.6	7.4	17.7	4.0	6.9	53.9	8.5	0.1
26. Other tobacco	7.6	29.6	21.1	13.7	15.8	11.9	0.4	0.4
27. Food products	3.7	14.2	10.2	6.2	12.6	49.4	3.8	1.1
28. Cotton textiles	3.0	11.6	8.2	6.1	17.2	50.6	3.3	0.7
29. Cotton yarn	3.0	11.6	8.2	6.1	17.2	50.6	3.3	0.8
30. Jute textiles	1.2	5.5	13.3	3.0	7.5	54.4	15.0	0.2
31. Woollen yarn	4.7	21.7	52.0	1.1	4.2	18.4	-2.1	0.1
32. Manmade fibres	0.1	0.5	1.1	7.8	16.0	57.9	16.6	0.1
33. Art silk fabrics	0.6	3.0	7.3	9.8	11.4	59.1	8.9	0.3
34. Silk and products	2.8	10.9	7.8	10.1	11.7	47.9	8.9	0.1
35. Other textiles	3.1	12.0	8.5	9.1	10.7	56.7	-0.1	0.2
36. Wood products	6.3	24.7	17.6	6.8	13.9	28.9	1.7	0.6
37. Paper and products	0.6	2.8	6.7	4.5	16.0	53.2	16.3	0.1
38. Leather footwear	2.9	11.3	8.1	8.9	18.3	45.3	5.2	0.1
39. Leather	2.6	11.8	28.4	6.2	12.7	36.0	2.3	0.1
40. Other leather products	5.6	21.7	15.5	6.9	14.1	34.0	2.3	0.1

Table 3.4 continued

Sector	Rural Bottom	Rural Middle	Rural Top	Urban Bottom	Urban Middle	Urban Top	Other Income	Sector share in total value added
41. Rubber products	0.6	2.7	6.6	3.4	7.4	61.6	17.7	0.2
42. Fertilisers	1.1	5.1	12.2	3.5	7.5	30.8	39.7	0.1
43. Chemicals	0.1	0.4	1.0	4.8	10.3	57.2	26.3	0.6
44. Plastics	0.6	2.7	6.4	6.5	13.6	50.9	19.3	0.1
45. Cosmetics and medicines	0.8	3.6	8.7	2.7	10.0	46.5	27.6	0.4
46. Petroleum products	0.0	0.2	0.5	0.1	3.6	30.6	65.0	0.2
47. Cement	2.4	11.1	26.6	1.2	5.1	34.6	19.1	0.2
48. Refractories	6.5	25.6	18.2	3.7	17.2	30.4	-1.7	0.5
49. Iron and steel	0.5	2.5	6.1	3.7	24.6	56.4	6.1	0.7
50. Non-ferrous metals	0.4	2.0	4.8	0.7	2.2	63.3	26.7	0.2
51. Metal products	1.2	4.7	3.3	4.4	13.8	66.1	6.5	0.9
52. Non-electrical machines	0.5	2.4	5.7	5.2	12.2	60.8	13.2	0.6
53. Electrical household goods	0.6	2.8	6.8	5.7	15.3	54.5	14.2	0.1
54. Radios	0.6	2.8	6.8	5.7	15.3	54.5	14.2	0.0
55. Other electrics	0.5	2.5	5.9	5.7	15.3	44.3	25.8	0.4
56. Bicycles	0.6	2.9	6.9	5.0	10.7	61.0	12.9	0.1
57. Motorcycles	0.5	2.4	5.7	4.4	11.4	62.8	12.9	0.0
58. Motor vehicles	0.5	2.4	5.7	4.4	11.4	62.8	12.9	0.4
59. Aircraft and ships	0.5	2.3	5.6	6.2	16.0	54.4	15.0	0.1
60. Railway equipment	0.5	2.2	5.3	5.3	27.7	40.9	18.0	0.3
61. O. trans. equipment	0.6	2.6	6.2	5.7	29.4	50.7	4.9	0.0
62. Watches and clocks	0.6	2.8	6.7	3.5	7.7	62.1	16.6	0.0
63. Miscellaneous scientific equipment	0.6	2.8	6.6	4.8	10.6	58.0	16.6	0.0
64. Other industries	0.6	2.7	6.4	5.6	11.9	53.4	19.5	0.1
65. Printing	0.6	2.7	6.5	9.9	21.2	40.3	18.9	0.2
66. Electricity	1.0	4.5	10.9	2.1	4.8	28.4	48.3	0.6
67. Rural housing	12.0	33.0	55.0	0.0	0.0	0.0	0.0	0.7
68. Urban housing	6.0	16.5	27.4	4.5	10.6	35.0	0.0	2.2
69. Other construction	6.0	16.5	27.4	4.5	10.6	35.0	0.0	0.9
70. Pucca construction	5.8	15.8	26.4	4.3	10.1	33.1	4.6	1.7
71. Railway transport	2.3	7.6	10.7	11.1	23.7	15.6	29.0	1.9
72. Other transport	3.5	11.7	16.5	15.8	17.8	20.0	14.7	2.2
73. Education	1.4	19.5	24.4	3.7	13.1	35.5	2.5	1.7
74. Entertainment	2.0	10.5	9.4	16.2	31.1	23.3	7.5	0.1
75. Medical care	0.8	10.8	13.6	5.1	18.1	49.2	2.5	0.6
76. Domestic service	2.9	15.7	14.0	15.5	29.6	22.2	0.0	0.3
77. Other services	8.6	25.5	17.6	3.8	10.2	31.7	2.5	22.5

Source : own estimates

Notes

1. In the 1967-8 Survey (NCAER, 1972) gross income of the household is defined as the sum of all earnings from self-employment in agriculture, business crafts, professions and services; salaries and wages including agricultural wages; rents from land and houses, interest and dividends, pensions and other incomes. The net income of each household is derived after deduction of depreciation. To obtain disposable income, allowance is made for non-agricultural income tax liability of the households. No other direct taxes (e.g. agricultural income tax) are taken into account. In the 1969 Survey (NCAER, 1975) only gross income of the households is reported.

2. See Bardhan (1974, pp. 106-12) for a detailed account and critique of these.

3. Mukherjee (1972) in his critique of the compilation of the national income accounts suggests that the output of a number of sectors (e.g. animal husbandry, small-scale industries, trade, household services) which together amount to some 40 per cent of aggregate NDP are estimated through a variety of indirect and subjective procedures. See also Mukherjee (1969, Appendix VIII, pp. 277-89).

4. For example, the NSS 1968-9 estimate of *per capita* consumption expenditure is 11 per cent lower than CSO. See Bardhan (1974, p. 116).

5. Bardhan mentions that there are some who suggest that it would be more appropriate to judge the validity of the CSO data by their proximity to NSS data! See, for instance, Rudra (1972).

6. The approximate lognormality of the NSS expenditure distribution has been established by a number of researchers; see Roy and Dhar (1960), Iyengar (1960a, 1960b), and Ahmed and Bhattacharya (1972).

7. If C follows a three-parameter lognormal distribution and $\log C = \alpha + \beta \log Y$, then $(\log C - \alpha)$ is $N\ (\theta, \sigma^2)$. Hence $\log Y$ is $N\ (\frac{\theta}{\beta}, \frac{\sigma^2}{\beta^2})$. Given the values of $\bar{C}$ and $\bar{Y}$ (average *per capita* consumption and disposable income, from CSO data, using NSS and NCAER rural/urban proportions) and β (elasticity of consumption w.r.t. income) the values of the following parameters are obtained:

$V\ (\log C) = \sigma^2$ is estimated directly from NSS grouped data.

$E\ (\log C) = \theta + \alpha$ is obtained by solving the expression:

$\bar{C} = e^{\theta + \alpha + \frac{1}{2}\sigma^2}$ for $\theta + \alpha$, since $\bar{C}$ and σ^2 are known.

$V\ (\log Y) = \frac{\sigma^2}{\beta^2}$ is calculated, since σ^2 and β are known.

$E\ (\log Y) = \frac{\theta}{\beta}$ is obtained by solving the expression:

$\bar{Y} = e^{\frac{\theta}{\beta} + \frac{1}{2}\frac{\sigma^2}{\beta^2}}$ for $\frac{\theta}{\beta}$, since $\frac{\sigma^2}{\beta^2}$ and $\bar{Y}$ are known.

α is then derived as a residual.

Lognormality of income distribution has been assumed by researchers concerned with other developing countries. See, for example, Adelman and Robinson (1978).

8. This tendency is apparent even in the distribution of consumption expenditure based on the NSS, where the estimates vary between 0.34 for 1958-9 and 0.29 for 1967-8.

9. The Indian Planning Commission comes to a similar conclusion for the 1950s, that the distribution of income in the rural sector seems to be less unequal than that in the urban sector (Government of India Planning Commission, 1964, Part I, p. 15).

10. The major explanations which have been suggested were discussed in Chapter 1.

11. Adelman and Robinson (1978, p. 27) were able to overcome this problem by carrying out a special household survey of the numbers of workers and their occupations.

12. A fuller account of the data sources and methods of allocation is given in Pearson and Pingle (1978).

13. The NCAER Rural Income Survey (NCAER, 1975) provides data on only six crops, rice, wheat, maize, jowar, cotton and sugarcane, while we distinguish 11 agricultural sectors. Moreover, the data there relate only to gross incomes from which it is not possible to derive value added.

14. For a detailed discussion of the concepts and measurement of gross output, business income and costs in the context of the FMS see Ganguli and Gupta (1976, especially pp. 254-5).

15. The sampling basis of the FMS has itself been criticised; see Saha (1975, pp. 113-22).

16. This would have been an all-India relationship only if the survey coverage of the states had been complete or at least representative. Furthermore, some of the surveys were not available to us and of those available only some permitted the calculation of *per capita* disposable income. Data from nine states were eventually used.

17. The bound between the bottom and middle classes lay at 2.20 ha, and between middle and top at 3.71 ha.

18. This regression was run on FMS data because the NCAER data were presented only on a per household and not a *per capita* basis. The bounds were 3.35 ha and 5.14 ha.

19. These figures were derived from FMS data by regressing household size against *per capita* income. Mean household sizes were 6.32 for the bottom class, 6.71 for the middle class and 7.79 for the top class, giving an overall mean of 6.94.

20. This is obviously a dubious assumption in view of the different crop pattern, higher wages and greater role of middlemen in urban areas. However, no more specific information was available.

21. The NCAER in its survey for 1967-8 derived the distribution as 96 per cent to 4 per cent (NCAER, 1972, Table 2, p. 62). Their income data, however, cover only the income of the self-employed, agricultural wages being grouped with general wages and salaries. Since most agricultural wages would be received in rural areas the NCAER figure may underestimate the rural share.

22. See Pillai (1975, p. 222); also Government of India NCA (1971, p. 39).

23. Data from NCA (1971).

24. Data from the IARS (ICAR) Surveys, with work animals assumed to be mainly in rural areas.

25. The division of each industry's value added between organised and unorganised sectors, and of the organised sector between the public and private sectors, was made largely on the basis of national accounts statistics (Government of India CSO, 1967, 1975, 1976), but occasionally on the less solid foundation of employment data from the Directorate General of Employment and Training. The separate wage and salary shares of public and private organised sectors were calculated by using ratios from the Annual Survey of Industries, 1967. Public sector retentions were derived as a residual share of public sector value added, after subtracting compensation of employees. Private organised sector retentions were obtained using proportions calculated from data on the finances of limited companies, from the Reserve Bank of India *Bulletin*, 1971. Corporate tax ratios were applied on the basis of data from all-India Income Tax Statistics. Distributions were derived as residuals, after subtracting all the other components of factor income listed above.

26. For one of the few studies of urban-rural income remittances, for Kenya, see Johnson and Whitelaw (1974).

27. Unregistered manufacturing units are those employing less than 10 workers, with the aid of power, or less than 20 workers, without the aid of power.

28. Government of India NSS (1975, 1976). The CSO also relies on NSS survey data in deriving some of its disaggregations; see Government of India CSO (1967, para. 3.1).

29. Initially we explored the possibility of building up the distribution of incomes from each industry from data on the occupational composition of the industry's workforce contained in publications of the Directorate General of Employment and Training (DGET) and estimates of average income by occupation from the NCAER and Labour Bureau. On the basis of its average earnings each occupational group was placed in one of our income classes. This method could not take account of the dispersion of earnings within any occupation and the number of occupational groups available (ten) was much too small to offset this limitation. Consequently the resulting distributions were implausible and were abandoned.

30. These surveys have since been repeated, but the results were not available in published form. The Labour Bureau was in fact willing to provide us with these results on punched cards, but their sheer volume made the processing of them beyond our resources.

31. An alternative procedure would have been to adopt the distribution found in single-industry centres to represent the industry; 98 per cent of manufacturing employment in Ahmedabad, for example, is in textiles. This procedure, however, would have made the resulting industry distributions vulnerable to specific local characteristics, including those attributable to sampling, while the elimination of centres with a plurality of industries would have involved considerable loss of information for larger cities.

32. CSO Brochure (Government of India CSO, 1967, pp. 57, 67, 74).

33. The distinction between labour- and capital-intensive industries, or between large and small scale cannot be made with any precision. An approximation, however, is given by the division between registered and unregistered enterprises. The CSO records the share of the registered sector in value added as 5 per cent in textiles, 29 per cent in wood products and 86 per cent in chemicals.

34. For other earlier estimates see Raj (1959), Rao (1965) and Mukherjee (1969).

4 ALTERNATIVE STRATEGIES OF INCOME REDISTRIBUTION

In the following three chapters we use the model to explore, through simulation, the implications of alternative strategies of income redistribution and growth for a range of macro-economic indicators: the level of personal incomes and their distribution across income classes and between rural and urban areas, the level and sectoral pattern of output, the provision of basic needs and the creation of employment. The focus of this chapter will be redistribution of income and we will consider a variety of income transfers between groups, from rich to poor both within and between rural and urban areas, including a transfer sufficient to meet basic needs. Chapter 5 then deals with employment, and Chapter 6 with growth.

Although the various policies simulated are focused either on income redistribution or on growth, the model has been designed to give an integrated treatment of the implications of any policy, both for output levels and for income distribution. Since the distribution of personal incomes among income classes is generated within the model at the level of the individual sector, a change in output in any sector is followed through to its impact on the distribution of personal incomes. And since the level and distribution of personal incomes determine consumption expenditure, any change there in turn affects sectoral output levels and, again, the distribution of income.

In simulating the impact of alternative developments our method is essentially that of comparative statics. A change introduced at any point in the model, for example by an income transfer, leads to successive changes in all the endogenous variables as the entire system adapts to the new values. This process continues until the income flow becomes self-replicating at a new level. This is then accepted as an equilibrium of the model and so as the representation of an equilibrium of the economy. Values from the new configuration are compared with those from the base configuration to give the implications of the policy change. Moreover, since the model is non-linear and solved by iteration round the circular flow of income, the iterative sequence itself can be interpreted in terms of the adjustment processes between positions of comparative-static equilibrium. Thus the iterative solution sequence provides insights into the process of income generation and distribution.

Income Flows within the Model

Before proceeding to the simulation of policy changes, however, it is
instructive to explore the properties of the model in its base equilibrium configuration. In particular, we will examine the inter-relationships among the income classes and the pattern of income flows which
are implied by the expenditure, output and distributional relations
specified in the model. We will trace the 'spillovers' of income, both
across income classes and between rural and urban areas, which result
from a notional increase of one rupee in the total income of an individual class, and also the consequent changes in consumption expenditure, sectoral outputs and incomes generated. The absolute income
changes are shown in Table 4.1, page 95, while in Table 4.2, page 97,
they are presented on a *per capita* basis.

In Table 4.1 each column shows the spillover of income to result,
for each class, from an income increase brought about by a notional
injection of one rupee to the total income of the specified class. Thus,
reading down the first column, a net income injection of one rupee
to the rural bottom class would result in an overall increase in personal
incomes of Rs 2.556, Rs 1.916 in rural areas and Re 0.640 in urban
areas. The recipient group itself derives spillover income of Re 0.213 in
addition to the injection; this represents the feedback to its own
income from both its own increment in expenditure and from the
expenditure of all the other groups out of their derived income
increases. The Re 1 income injection to the rural bottom class implies a
slightly greater income increase, Rs 1.183, for the rural top class,
around half of that, Re 0.520, for the rural middle class and smaller
amounts for the urban groups. Both the total amount of the spillovers
and their distribution among the various classes are determined by the
overall structure of the system and the positions of the individual
groups within it. In order to give an intuitive understanding of the
economic forces at work, we will trace through the main features of the
spillover process in the case of an increase in income for the rural poor.

First, however, we re-examine certain characteristics of the rural
poor: their average income is less than that required to meet their basic
needs; as a group they dissave on the average, and their overall marginal
propensity to consume out of disposable income is virtually unity.
Seventy-eight per cent of their total expenditure is on food, particularly
rice, the minor foodgrains (barley, millet, etc.) and vegetables; among
the commodities which feature significantly in their expenditure
pattern, all are 'luxuries', with Engel elasticities exceeding unity, except
for other foodgrains (0.47) and, marginally, rice (0.96). It follows that

if the incomes of the rural poor are raised, almost the entire increment is spent, predominantly on food. However, the pattern of incomes generated in the agricultural sectors is heavily skewed in favour of the top income group in the rural areas, who receive 72 per cent of the incomes, against 12 per cent for the rural poor and 14 per cent for the middle income group.[1] The expenditure pattern of the rural poor thus immediately creates a major spillover of income to the top rural group. This group has the lowest marginal propensity to consume of all the groups. In their consumption basket agricultural products still absorb more than half of total expenditure, but the Engel elasticities for the various crop products are substantially lower than those of the poorer classes, while animal products are much more important. Manufactures, notably food products, textiles and footwear, absorb 36 per cent of expenditure, while services such as transport, education, medical and domestic services become much more prominent. Their high marginal propensity to save makes the feedback flows of income relatively small. The still sizeable position of agricultural products in their expenditure pattern means that, to a significant extent, expenditure by the rural rich generates incomes in the rural areas, most notably for themselves as a group, but with the incomes generated in animal husbandry particularly benefiting the rural middle class. On the other hand, purchases of manufactures and, to a lesser extent, services by the rural rich create a substantial spillover of income to the urban groups and particularly to the urban top class. Part of this, in turn, flows back to the rural areas through urban demand for food and other primary products from the rural areas.

The income changes recorded for the various groups thus encapsulate the implications for their income position of the sequence of income and expenditure changes which result from a Re 1 increase in the income of the rural poor as a group. The process of the spillover of income across groups is thus a complex one, involving in the first instance the group's own marginal consumption pattern and then, through the resultant distribution of income, the expenditure patterns of all groups and the consequent flows of incomes generated. Where the expenditure patterns or the resulting income distribution are strongly skewed, the leading influences can be identified, but even these are partially overlaid by feedback effects from further adjustments. Rather than trace through the sequence of adjustment following an income increase for each group[2] we will concentrate our discussion on some of the leading general features of the pattern of income spillovers.

Table 4.1: Spillovers of Income among Classes and between Rural and Urban Areas

	Income increase from injection of Re 1					
	Rural			Urban		
Income groups	Bottom	Middle	Top	Bottom	Middle	Top
Rural						
Bottom	0.213	0.241	0.193	0.174	0.227	0.169
Middle	0.520	0.659	0.554	0.483	0.657	0.496
Top	1.183	1.141	0.866	1.029	1.084	0.787
Total rural	1.916	2.041	1.613	1.686	1.968	1.452
Urban						
Bottom	0.065	0.089	0.078	0.069	0.096	0.077
Middle	0.161	0.230	0.202	0.166	0.244	0.193
Top	0.414	0.602	0.531	0.415	0.627	0.490
Total urban	0.640	0.921	0.811	0.650	0.967	0.760
Total spillovers	2.556	2.962	2.424	2.336	2.935	2.212

An income change for any group has spillover effects on all group incomes, including its own, but the size of these differs markedly. The largest spillover effects result from income increases for the rural middle class and the urban middle class. This is, at first sight, a surprising finding, since it might be expected that the multiplier effects would be greatest through the poorest groups, where the marginal propensity to consume is highest. It is certainly the case in our model that the poor have higher marginal propensities to consume than the middle income groups (0.98 against 0.77 in rural areas, 0.95 against 0.78 in urban areas), bringing a higher first-round spillover effect. But in the expenditure patterns of the bottom groups the purchase of food plays a more dominant role, resulting in the generation of incomes for the rural top class with its relatively low marginal propensity to consume. The spillover effects working through the expenditure patterns and consequent distribution of incomes thus outweigh the direct impact of a differentially higher marginal propensity to consume. This is one of the more striking instances of the importance of incorporating the feedback effects through the sectoral distribution of incomes, the results from a closed model reversing those derivable from reasoning along the lines of an open model.

The income spillovers to both the rural and urban poor from an increase in income of any of the richer classes are fairly small; Re 1 of

additional income given to another class implies only between Re
0.169 and Re 0.241 for the rural poor and between Re 0.065 and Re
0.096 for the urban poor. Not only is this a small amount in absolute
terms but it is invariably smaller than the spillover derived by the
corresponding middle or top income class. The reason for this is the
very low share in value added from any sector which goes to either the
rural or the urban poor; since in every sector group their share is less
than that received by the middle and top groups there is no change in
income, and so in the pattern of demand and output, which benefits them
significantly. It is, however, significant, particularly from a policy
point of view, that in each case they benefit more through spillovers
from an income increase for the middle groups than for the top groups.

The spillovers to the rural top group, on the other hand, are invariably substantial. In particular, with values between Rs 1.029 and Rs
1.183 they gain more income simply through spillovers than the Re 1
received as an injection by the rural bottom or middle classes or the
urban bottom or middle classes. A Re 1 income injection to rural top
brings them a further Re 0.866 in spillovers, a much higher rate of
reinforcement of the injection than for any other group. The spillovers to the rural top group are of fundamental significance for the
implications revealed by the model simulations. The dominant forces
bringing them about are the high proportion of any increment in income
received by the poor (and, to a lesser extent, the rich) which is spent
on food, combined with the highly skewed distribution of agricultural
incomes, with its bias towards the rural top class.

The impact of the spillovers on the relative positions of the rural
and urban areas and of the various income groups emerges clearly
when the spillovers are converted to a *per capita* basis (and scaled for
absolute size). Where in absolute size the rural spillovers are two or
even three times greater than the urban spillovers (Table 4.1), Table
4.2, page 97, shows that on a *per capita* basis the spillover incomes
received in urban areas, on the average and class by class, are
invariably greater than those in the rural areas. Even in the most
favourable case, the income injection to the rural bottom class, the
average spillover income received per head in the rural areas is only 70
per cent of that received in the urban areas. The first-round rural
orientation of expenditure through the dominance of agricultural
products is followed by a major income spillover to the rural rich and
so to the urban areas; although the actual income flows to the urban
areas are much smaller than those remaining in the rural areas, they are
insufficient to offset the population differential, so giving rise to the

urban bias when the spillovers are measured on a *per capita* basis.[3] In both rural and urban areas the evolving expenditure pattern as income rises brings an urban bias in the *per capita* spillovers which increases considerably with income.

Table 4.2: *Per Capita* Spillovers of Income among Classes and between Rural and Urban Areas*

| | Per capita income increase from injection of Re 1 to | | | | | |
| | Rural | | | Urban | | |
Income groups	Bottom	Middle	Top	Bottom	Middle	Top
Rural						
Bottom	1.579	1.786	1.430	1.289	1.682	1.252
Middle	3.740	4.740	3.985	3.474	4.726	3.568
Top	8.767	8.456	6.418	7.626	8.033	5.832
Average rural	4.686	4.991	3.945	4.123	4.813	3.551
Urban						
Bottom	2.020	2.766	2.424	2.144	2.984	2.393
Middle	4.856	6.938	6.093	5.007	7.360	5.822
Top	12.867	18.710	16.503	12.898	19.487	15.229
Average urban	6.564	9.446	8.318	6.667	9.918	7.795
Average spillover	5.047	5.849	4.787	4.613	5.796	4.368
Average rural as % of average urban	70	53	47	62	49	46

*All figures have been scaled up by 10^9.

Among the classes individually, the bias in the spillovers in favour of the top class in rural areas, which was so striking in terms of absolute income flows, is clearly exceeded on a *per capita* basis by the spillovers to the urban top class. Thus, while income flows to the rural top class are of major importance because of the size of this class and its role in creating income spillovers from rural to urban areas, the income spillovers to the urban top class are of particular significance in terms of the skewness of the overall distribution of incomes. Furthermore, as with the absolute spillovers, the highest rural, urban and all-India average spillovers result from injections to the rural and urban middle classes.

The patterns of these various income flows, and the forces giving rise to them, are fundamental to the implications which the model will reveal for alternative policies of income redistribution or economic growth. We turn now to the simulation of various possible strategies, first for income redistribution and then for growth.

Once-for-All Redistribution

A simple exercise, but one which is highly instructive in revealing the properties of the model, is the simulation of the consequences of a once-for-all transfer of income from one group to another. It is, of course, well known, by exact analogy with the 'one shot' investment multiplier, that a once-for-all income transfer will not result in any sustained change in the level or configuration of incomes.[4] However, by tracing the resulting sequence of income flows through the model, the processes through which income returns to its initial configuration are identified in terms of the relationships and parameters of the model.

The redistribution which we simulate here is the transfer from the top income group in rural areas to the rural poor, of a lump sum *per capita*, equivalent to a 10 per cent increase in the *per capita* income of the poor, from Rs 171 to Rs 188. The income situation of each class and the employment implications at various rounds or iterations of the model are shown in Table 4.3, page 99. The initial levels of *per capita* income (column 1) are the base values of the model. In round 1 the incomes of the rural poor are increased by Rs 17 per head, and those of the rural rich correspondingly reduced; all other incomes remain unaltered.

In round 2, as the rural poor spend their increased income and the rich adjust to the reduction in theirs, the new pattern and volume of demand give rise to a configuration of incomes in which the poor have already lost Rs 16.9 out of the Rs 17.1 transferred to them initially. The rich, on the other hand, gain back almost Rs 21.9 against their initial loss, through the transfer, of only Rs 17.1. All the other groups have suffered a slight loss of income.

Two factors give rise to this immediate, and virtually complete, erosion of the income transfer initially given to the poor. First, the extra income is immediately spent, predominantly on agricultural products from which the poor as a class receive only a low share in value added; this factor alone would reduce their income retained at the end of the round to about Rs 2. In addition to this, moreover, the loss of income suffered by the rich brings a significant reduction in demand for food, still their largest single item of expenditure, and consequently a loss to the poor of their share in that part of value added which would otherwise have been created.

Table 4.3: Once-for-all Redistribution from Rural Top to Rural Bottom: Initial Transfer of Rs 17.09 *per Capita* (Rs *per capita*)

Income groups	Initial income levels	Income at round 1	Income at round 2	Income at equilibrium
Rural				
Bottom	171.0	188.1	171.2	171.0
Middle	376.3	376.3	375.4	376.3
Top	942.3	925.2	947.1	942.4
Gini coefficient	0.344	0.329	0.345	0.344
Urban				
Bottom	234.1	234.1	233.1	234.1
Middle	540.5	540.5	537.3	540.4
Top	1442.7	1442.7	1433.4	1442.6
Gini coefficient	0.363	0.363	0.362	0.363
Total employment (millions)	94.72	94.79	94.74	94.72

The gain in income by the rich in round 2 is at least as striking as the erosion of the advantage received by the poor. The net increase, in addition to the recouping of the transfer, results from the differing overall marginal propensities to consume of the two groups. The poor, who dissave on average, have a marginal propensity to consume only fractionally below unity; the rural rich, on the other hand, are substantial savers, both on average and at the margin. The income transfer thus increases the overall level of demand as well as the bias towards agricultural products, where over 70 per cent of the income generated is received by the rural rich. The fall in incomes for all three urban classes reflects the lower levels of expenditure by the rural rich in response to the income transfer.

Further adjustments, now of relatively small size, continue through subsequent rounds. The increased income received by the rural rich in round 2 raises the incomes of the other groups in the next round, but falls itself as the boost from the expenditure of the rural poor is not repeated, so bringing further adjustments of diminishing size until all income levels have reconverged at their initial values. Employment follows total expenditure in rising initially with the income transfer then falling back to its original level.

Two striking features seem to emerge from this description of a straightforward, once-for-all transfer of income from rich to poor. The first is the pervasiveness and complexity of the repercussions, involving all income classes in a sequence of income gains and losses as levels and patterns of both expenditures and incomes adjust. Perhaps most striking of all is the speed and completeness with which the income advantage given to the poor is wiped out by the structural forces within the system.

Effective Redistribution of Income

It was inevitable that a once-for-all income transfer should bring only a temporary improvement in the income position of the poor and the level of employment. Of much greater significance, in terms of policy implications, is a redistribution of income where the target group is raised to, and then maintained at, a higher level of income. The objective in our second set of simulations is to explore the nature and implications of the redistribution required for this. Since, as the previous simulation showed, an income transfer from the rich to the poor is largely reversed almost immediately by the system itself, in the current exercise the income retained by the target group at the end of each round is augmented by whatever further transfer is necessary to bring them to a level of Rs 10 *per capita* above their pre-redistribution position. This process of replacing the amount eroded from the income transfer is continued until a new configuration of income levels is reached at which the incomes of all classes are constant, with the target group Rs 10 per head above its base level and the transfer being made at a constant rate in every round. In this new equilibrium, the income transfer will typically not be exactly equal to the Rs 10 *per capita* gained by the target group, because of the impact on their incomes of the spillovers brought about by the redistribution itself. Similarly, through spillovers the income redistribution will affect the incomes of all other groups, in addition to those directly involved in the transfer. The changes in the level and distribution of income will in turn affect the level of employment. The results of this exercise are summarised in Tables 4.4 and 4.5, pages 101, 102; each income class in turn is treated as the target group, with the income transfers coming respectively from the rural and urban top classes.

In any redistribution two sets of adjustments are introduced simultaneously, those associated with the income increase for the target group and those associated with the income reduction for the class from which the transfer is taken. The income change for each class is the net result of these two overlaying sets of effects. In the case of an income transfer to the rural bottom from the rural top, in the equilibrium configuration of incomes where the *per capita* income of the rural poor has been increased by Rs 10, the maintained transfer, at Rs 9.79 *per capita*, is slightly less than the increase in income achieved by the target group. Thus the net effect on them of the various spillovers is positive; they gain more through the spillovers to themselves from the income transfer than they lose through spillovers from the income reduction which the transfer causes to the rural top class.[5] The spillovers are even more conspicuously positive in the case of the rural rich.

Table 4.4: Effective Redistribution: Income Transfer from Rural Top Class Ensuring Rs 10 Increase for Target Group

Income groups	Initial per capita income (Rs)	Equilibrium income (Rs) resulting from income transfer to				
		Rural bottom	Rural middle	Urban bottom	Urban middle	Urban top
Rural						
Bottom	171.0	181.0 (+)[a]	171.4 (+)	170.9 (−)	171.1 (+)	170.9 (−)
Middle	376.3	376.0 (−)	386.3 (+)	376.2 (−)	376.6 (+)	376.2 (−)
Top	942.3	935.6 (−)	935.5 (−)	940.3 (−) (933.8)[b]	940.5 (−) (934.5)	939.7 (−) (931.1)
All rural	495.3	496.3 (+)	496.6 (+)	494.6 (−)	494.9 (−)	494.4 (−)
Rural Gini coefficient	0.344	0.330	0.329	0.343	0.342	0.337
Urban						
Bottom	234.1	233.6 (−)	234.6 (+)	244.1 (+)	234.3 (+)	234.1 (0)
Middle	540.5	538.9 (−)	541.6 (+)	540.2 (−)	550.5 (+)	540.4 (+)
Top	1442.7	1438.2 (−)	1445.7 (+)	1441.7 (−)	1443.8 (+)	1452.7 (+)
All urban	737.1	734.9 (−)	738.6 (+)	740.0 (+)	740.9 (+)	740.4 (+)
Urban Gini coefficient	0.363	0.362	0.363	0.352	0.354	0.381
Transfer received						
Initial	−	10.00	10.00	10.00	10.00	10.00
Equilibrium[c]	−	9.79	9.03	10.09	9.57	10.33
Employment[d]	94.715	94.800	94.936	94.703	94.765	94.694

a. (+) indicates a rise in income, (0) no change, and (−) a fall, compared with initial values.
b. Figures in parentheses show incomes which the rural top group would have retained if the urban population had been the same size as the rural population.
c. The equilibrium transfers do not equal Rs 10 because of spillover effects. The size of the transfer cannot be calculated directly from this table.
d. Employment is measured in millions of man years.

Table 4.5: Effective Redistribution: Income Transfer from Urban Top
Class Ensuring Rs 10 Increase for Target Group

Income groups	Initial per capita income (Rs)	Equilibrium income (Rs) resulting from income transfer to				
		Rural bottom	Rural middle	Rural top	Urban bottom	Urban middle
Rural						
Bottom	171.0	181.0 (+)[a]	171.6 (+)	171.2 (+)	171.0 (0)	171.1 (+)
Middle	376.3	376.5 (+)	386.3 (+)	376.8 (+)	376.3 (0)	376.7 (+)
Top	942.3	946.2 (+)	945.5 (+)	952.3 (+)	942.9 (+)	943.0 (+)
All rural	495.3	500.0 (+)	500.0 (+)	498.9 (+)	495.5 (+)	495.7 (+)
Rural Gini coefficient	0.344	0.338	0.342	0.346	0.345	0.344
Urban						
Bottom	234.1	233.6 (−)	234.5 (+)	234.1 (0)	244.1 (+)	234.3 (+)
Middle	540.5	539.2 (−)	541.7 (+)	540.7 (+)	540.2 (−)	550.5 (+)
Top	1442.7	1399.6 (−) (1432.4)	1409.4 (−) (1434.8)	1405.5 (−) (1433.8)[b]	1431.9 (−)	1434.3 (−)
All urban	737.1	722.3 (−)	726.7 (−)	724.9 (−)	736.7 (−)	737.8 (+)
Urban Gini coefficient	0.363	0.357	0.358	0.357	0.348	0.348
Transfer received						
Initial	--	10.00	10.00	10.00	10.00	10.00
Equilibrium[c]	--	9.56	8.63	9.22	10.08	9.51
Employment[d]	94.715	94.884	95.002	94.797	94.724	94.785

a. (+) indicates a rise in income, (0) no change, and (−) a fall, compared with initial values.
b. Figures in parentheses show incomes which the urban rich would have retained if the rural population had been the same (smaller) size as the urban population.
c. The equilibrium transfers do not equal Rs 10 because of spillover effects.
d. Employment is measured in million man years.

Their new equilibrium income, Rs 935.6, is only Rs 6.7 below its original level, even after they pay the transfer of Rs 9.79; before paying the transfer it is Rs 945.4, Rs 3.1 *above* its pre-redistribution level. Thus the net spillover to the rich from the process of redistribution (Rs 3.1) is equivalent to three-tenths of the transfer which they must pay. Only seven-tenths of the transfer and, correspondingly, a slightly smaller proportion of the income increase of Rs 10 for the target group, is a 'cost' to the rural rich, in terms of the actual reduction in their income. The net effect of the redistribution on the other four classes, however, is negative; they lose more from the income reduction experienced by the rural rich than they gain from the income increase to the rural poor.

Since, aside from the transfers themselves, these effects all derive as spillovers, the mechanisms giving rise to them are essentially those discussed above. The transfer of income from rich to poor brings about, through the higher marginal propensity to consume of the poor, a higher level of expenditure and so of incomes generated, which tends to give rise initially to income increases for all groups. The redistribution also brings a shift within the expenditure pattern towards agricultural products where the share of the rural rich in value added is particularly high. Through this channel the rural rich regain part of the income which they lose in the transfer. Their net loss of income through the transfer is the major factor reducing the incomes of the urban groups.

A more complete, but mechanistic rather than descriptive, analysis of the impact of the redistribution can be made directly by applying the per rupee estimates of the spillovers given in Table 4.1 to the positive and negative income 'injections' involved in the transfer. The positive net spillover effect of the redistribution on the income of the rural bottom class found in the simulation can be viewed (or 'explained') as the net effect from a spillover to itself of Re 0.213 per rupee of income transfer against a spillover loss of Re 0.193 per rupee of income lost by the rural top class. The positive spillovers to the rural top class implied in an equilibrium reduction in net income of less than the amount of the transfer is again to be expected from a gain per rupee of transfer, of Rs 1.183 against a loss of Re 0.866. The net spillover effects on the other four groups follow similarly.

The redistribution of income from the rural top class to the rural middle class is markedly different in its effects from a redistribution to the rural poor. The necessary *per capita* transfer received from the rural rich is, at Rs 9.03, significantly lower than for the rural poor and indeed lower than is received by any other group. This reflects the fact that the level of spillover back to itself from an income increase is higher in the case of the rural middle class than of any other group, except rural top (Table 4.1). Moreover, the spillovers from the rural middle group to the rural poor and to all the urban classes are higher than the spillovers to these groups from the rural rich. Hence, by contrast with the redistribution in favour of the rural poor, redistribution to the rural middle class from the rural rich has a favourable effect on the incomes of all the other groups.

When income redistribution is made in favour of the urban classes, the most striking feature is that for both the bottom and top classes the necessary transfer (at Rs 10.09, and Rs 10.33, respectively) from the rural rich exceeds the income improvement gained by the target group. The net spillover effects are negative, in that the urban poor gain more, per rupee, and *per capita* per rupee, from the marginal expenditure pattern of the rural rich than from their own. Moreover, the spillover effects of an income transfer from rural rich to urban poor are negative for all groups except the rural rich. The transfer implies a reduction in income for all groups except the recipients; the amount of the necessary transfer, Rs 10.33, exceeds the income improvement for the urban poor and, if the urban population had not been much smaller than the rural population, would have cost the rural rich yet more in lost income. (The figures in parentheses in Table 4.4 indicate the incomes which the rural rich would have retained if the urban population had been of equal size to the rural population.) With a redistribution from the rural top to the urban middle class, on the other hand, all the spillover effects are positive, as they were in the case of a redistribution in favour of the rural middle class.

Similar results in the case of an income transfer from the top urban class to all the others are shown in Table 4.5. Again the spillover effects on the target group are typically positive, with the urban bottom class a conspicuous, though marginal, exception. The same policy dilemma emerges as in the case of transfers from the rural top class, that with a redistribution to the rural poor the urban poor lose, although in this case a redistribution to the urban poor leaves the rural poor fractionally better off. Again as with redistribution from the rural top class, income transfers to either middle class have positive spillover effects on all income groups, and sometimes substantially so. The redistribution of income in favour of the middle class, and in particular the rural middle class, also achieves the greatest increase in employment.

We have reported simulation results only for income transfers from the top rural and urban classes to all the others, but the summary of the spillover effects given in Tables 4.1 and 4.2 allows the direction and approximate magnitude of the change from any other redistribution to be estimated.

Doubling Incomes of the Poor

The redistribution of income in favour of the poor must be assessed as
a major policy option because of its implications for the provision of
basic needs, even although its impact on the overall distribution of
income and the level of employment are not entirely favourable. As we
discussed above,[6] there is considerable diversity in the estimates of the
income levels required to meet basic needs, and on all but the most
austere measures these are unattainable in India even with an equal
per capita share-out of total current national income. As a compromise, therefore, between what is necessary and what is feasible, we
simulate the impact of a doubling of the *per capita* incomes of the rural
and the urban poor by redistribution from the top class in their respective areas. The doubling of the average *per capita* income of the poor,
from Rs 171 to Rs 342 in rural areas and from Rs 234 to Rs 468 in
urban areas, places them clearly in the middle income group, but still
9 per cent and 13 per cent respectively below the mean income levels
there. The implication of doubling the incomes of the poor, for the
income levels of all groups, the distribution of incomes and the level
of employment are shown in Table 4.6, page 106. The rural and urban
redistributions, as well as the combined effects of redistribution in both
areas together,[7] are given separately in order to show the differing
patterns of their effects.

Doubling the average *per capita* income of the rural poor by income
transfer brings a reduction in the incomes of the rural rich of 13 per
cent. The poor approximately double their share in total personal incomes, from 8.4 per cent to 16.5 per cent, while the share of the rural
rich falls from 46.3 per cent to 39.6 per cent. Again, through the operation of spillovers, the cost of the transfer to the rural rich is significantly
less than appears initially. The incomes of the bottom group represent
18 per cent of the base value of the income of rural top but with the
changes in expenditure and incomes consequent on the redistribution,
they regain sufficient income to reduce their net loss to 13 per cent.
Personal incomes rise in total by 1.75 per cent as a result of the redistribution, but in spite of this the spillover effects bring an actual reduction in the incomes of all the urban classes. Thus, apart from the target
group, whose position is substantially improved, all the other groups
except, very marginally, the rural middle class, are adversely affected
by the redistribution. However, the increased level of personal incomes
and the shift in the expenditure pattern consequent on the redistribution
causes employment to rise by 2 per cent, more than the increase in incomes, but still, in view of the size of the redistribution, not a substantial improvement.[8]

Table 4.6: Doubling the Incomes of the Bottom Classes through
Transfers from the Top Classes

A. Transfer to the Rural Bottom Class from the Rural Top Class

	Initial per capita income (Rs)	Initial income share (%)	New per capita income (Rs)	New income share (%)	Change in income (%)
Rural					
Bottom	171.0	8.4	341.9	16.5	+100.0
Middle	376.3	19.1	377.1	18.8	+ 0.2
Top	942.3	46.3	819.0	39.6	− 13.1
Urban					
Bottom	234.1	2.7	230.6	2.7	− 1.5
Middle	540.5	6.5	528.0	6.3	− 2.3
Top	1442.7	16.9	1405.1	16.2	− 2.6
Total personal incomes (thousand million Rs)	274.410	100	279.222	100	+ 1.75
Total employment (million)	94.72		96.48		+ 1.86

B. Transfer to the Urban Bottom Class from the Urban Top Class

	Initial per capita income (Rs)	Initial income share (%)	New per capita income (Rs)	New income share (%)	Change in income (%)
Rural					
Bottom	171.0	8.4	170.6	8.4	− 0.2
Middle	376.3	19.1	374.4	19.0	− 0.5
Top	942.3	46.3	950.8	46.8	+ 0.9
Urban					
Bottom	234.1	2.7	468.2	5.5	+100.0
Middle	540.5	6.5	533.8	6.5	− 1.2
Top	1442.7	16.9	1187.2	13.9	− 17.7
Total personal incomes (thousand million Rs)	274.410	100	274.331	100	− 0.03
Total employment (million)	94.72		94.60		− 0.001

C. Simultaneous Transfer to Both Rural and Urban Poor[a]

	Initial per capita income (Rs)	Initial income share (%)	New per capita income (Rs)	New income share (%)	Change in income (%)
Rural:					
Bottom	171.0	8.4	341.9	16.6	+ 100
Middle	376.3	19.1	374.8	18.7	− 0.004
Top	942.3	46.3	824.6	39.9	− 12.5
Gini coefficient		0.344		0.208	
Urban					
Bottom	234.1	2.7	468.2	5.4	+100
Middle	540.5	6.5	521.1	6.2	− 0.036
Top	1442.7	16.9	1145.3	13.2	− 20.6
Gini coefficient		0.363		0.211	
Total personal incomes (thousand million Rs)	274.410	100	278.702	100	+ 1.56
Total employment (million)	94.72		96.21		+ 1.59

a. This result combines *A* and *B* (above); interaction between the two transfers
   produces a slightly different configuration of incomes.

In the case of a redistribution to the urban poor the associated changes are even more adverse. Total personal incomes and employment actually fall, although by very small amounts. Apart from the urban poor the only group to gain an increase in income are the rural rich; since at the same time the rural poor suffer a reduction in their incomes, the urban redistribution brings a significant worsening of the overall distribution of incomes in the rural areas. As far as incomes and employment are concerned, therefore, there are no incidental or subsidiary benefits to be derived from the redistribution.

The implications for output and employment in individual sector groups from the doubling of the incomes of the poor through income transfers, as shown in Table 4.7, page 108, are much as would be expected. The most marked increases are in agriculture and food products where the improved income position of the poor leads to increases in output of 7.9 and 8.9 per cent respectively, with a corresponding increase of 7.3 per cent in man years of employment in agriculture. Manufacturing output as a whole increases by 3.2 per cent but manufacturing employment by only 1.4 per cent.

Perhaps the most striking aspects of these estimates is the relatively small extent of the adjustments to output, employment and incomes, other than those of the target group, implied by the redistribution. For the poor the change involved is massive, but the net reduction in the incomes of the rural and urban rich together is slightly less than 15 per cent. Even in those sector groups where the main impact of the higher incomes of the poor is felt through demand for agricultural and food products, the necessary increases in output are only 8-9 per cent and under 6 per cent in animal husbandry, even for a simultaneous doubling of the incomes of both the rural and the urban poor. This limited impact has both positive and negative aspects. The relatively small increase in the demand for agricultural and food products is of great practical significance in a situation where food supplies may be regarded as a bottle-neck in attempts to reduce poverty.[9] On the other hand, the limited impact on output brings an even smaller impact on employment. Hence the employment potential of income redistribution, even on this scale, is negligible.

Simulation results with various patterns of income redistribution thus confirm what acceptance of the necessity of a closed model of income distribution made likely; that the distribution of incomes results from a complex interaction of expenditure patterns and income shares, and that the implications of income redistribution are extensive and diverse, and not accurately predicted by reference to a few simple

Table 4.7: Output and Employment Changes, by Sector Group, when Incomes of the Poor are Doubled (Figures in parentheses are percentage changes)

	Output (Rs)[a] with redistribution				Employment (million) with redistribution			
	Initial level	Rural only	Urban only	Simultaneous transfers to both rural and urban	Initial level	Rural only	Urban only	Simultaneous transfers to both rural and urban
Agriculture	142.4	152.1 (+6.8)	144.3 (+1.3)	153.6 (+7.9)	45.7	48.7 (+6.6)	46.2 (+0.9)	49.0 (+7.3)
Animal husbandry	27.3	28.3 (+3.8)	27.8 (+1.9)	28.8 (+5.5)	2.8	2.9[b] (+3.6)[b]	2.9[b] (+1.8)[b]	3.0 (+5.4)
Total primary	178.3	189.2 (+6.1)	180.7 (+1.4)	191.1 (+7.2)	49.7	52.8 (+6.3)	50.2 (+1.0)	53.2 (+7.0)
Food products	37.2	39.7 (+6.8)	38.0 (+2.3)	40.5 (+8.9)	3.7	3.8 (+2.5)	3.7 (+0.5)	3.8 (+2.7)
Textiles and footwear	25.5	25.8 (+1.5)	25.7 (+0.9)	26.0 (+2.0)	5.7	5.8 (+1.4)	5.7 (+0.7)	5.8 (+1.4)
Total manufacturing	127.0	130.3 (+2.6)	128.0 (+0.8)	131.1 (+3.2)	16.5	16.7 (+1.2)	16.6 (+0.4)	16.7 (+1.4)
Services (excluding other services)	67.3	67.8 (+0.8)	67.3 (+0.1)	67.8 (+0.7)	9.4	9.5 (+0.8)	9.5 (+0.6)	9.6 (+1.8)
All sectors	436.5	445.8 (+2.1)	437.6 (+0.2)	446.1 (+2.2)	94.7	96.5 (+1.9)	94.6 (−0.1)	96.2 (+1.6)

a. Output is gross output, measured in thousand million rupees.

b. These figures need a word of caution. Although the two absolute figures are the same, percentage increases given in parentheses are very different. This arises from the fact that these percentages were calculated from the detailed results, while the absolute figures expressed here are rounded figures.

parameters such as the differing marginal propensities to consume of various groups. In particular, any redistribution of income affects all groups in the economy, sometimes favourably and sometimes unfavourably, and to widely differing degrees. The redistributional pattern which has most favourable effects on incomes and employment is redistribution from the rich to the middle income groups. Redistribution from the rich to the poor, on the other hand, does not have unambiguously favourable consequences. Income transfers to the rural poor do little to benefit the urban poor, while transfers to the urban poor actually reduce the incomes of the rural poor and simultaneously increase those of the rural rich. The only marked changes in the output pattern required by the redistributions are for agricultural and food products, and even here the net increase is not great. The sensitivity of employment to income redistribution is even more limited, and in the case of a reduction in urban poverty the response is actually negative; hence there is only very limited scope for increasing employment while manipulating the income distribution towards meeting basic needs.

Change in the Structure of Income Shares: a Simulated Land Redistribution

The redistributions discussed so far have consisted in income transfers between classes, within the given structure of group shares in value added at the sectoral level. An alternative, and more fundamental, form of redistribution would be the redistribution of assets, to change the income shares accruing from production to the various classes. To explore the implications of such a change we have run our model with the shares in agricultural incomes completely equalised, in place of the previous highly skewed distribution, as might result from a radical land redistribution. Such a change is of substantive as well as analytical interest, in that it makes a major contribution towards the implementation of a basic needs strategy for the rural poor, through providing them with a greatly increased volume of assets and, consequently, level of income.

Before reporting the results of these simulations it is instructive to examine the extent of land redistribution which would be required to meet basic needs. We begin by estimating roughly the amount of land needed per person to meet a requirement of 2,250 calories, three-quarters of which are obtained from cereals and pulses. Under these circumstances, the protein requirement is automatically met. No other requirement, such as a minimum availability of vitamins, is imposed. Furthermore, no provision is made for animal foods,[10] although some allowance is made for items like edible oil and sugar. A further allowance is made for non-food expenditure. Under these assumptions, an average person in India would require (at 1966-8 levels of agricultural productivity) 0.38 ha. of land, in order to meet basic needs at an austerity level.

The total amount of arable land in India in the mid-1960s was approximately 165 million ha. This means that the *per capita* availability of land (for the rural population only) would be just over 0.38 ha. It follows that only something approaching complete equality of land ownership would provide enough land to the rural poor to enable them to approach the fulfilment of their basic needs at the austerity level; this will ensure only a survival standard of living, and not a reasonable basic minimum. An income level which could ensure such a reasonable minimum will continue to be out of their reach.

This simulation, in which value added in agriculture is equally distributed, can therefore be regarded as one which approximates the consequences of a redistribution of agricultural land, designed to help the poor to meet their basic needs. It is necessarily a very rough approximation, since it is almost impossible to anticipate or to quantify the likely changes in cropping pattern and input use (particularly as between family and hired labour) which would follow from such a major modification in the social and economic structure. As such, the results of this simulation have to be viewed with caution.

The simulation results are summarised in Table 4.8, page 111. The most striking results are the dramatic improvement in the income positions of the poor and the middle income groups in the rural areas. The *per capita* income of the rural poor is more than doubled, as is their share in total personal incomes. Both the *per capita* income level and the income share of the middle group are increased by more than half. The rural top class, on the other hand, suffer a loss of one-third in incomes and income share. These changes reflect strongly the importance of agricultural incomes for the rural population and in particular for the lower income groups. In urban areas, where agriculture is not a major source of income, the resultant changes are small. With these distributional changes, total personal incomes rise by 7.4 per cent, and gross output by 6.8 per cent.[11]

Substantial though the changes are, even complete equalisation of shares in the income generated in agriculture still leaves even rural incomes significantly unequally distributed. Although land is the major asset in rural areas, unequal ownership of other assets, physical and human, still maintains inequality of incomes.[12]

Total employment rises by 7.3 per cent suggesting, at first sight, that the employment-creating potential of even a completely equal land redistribution is rather limited. Hence, if employment creation were a prime objective, land redistribution is possibly not a very effective instrument with which to promote it.[13] This may not be a valid conclusion, however. A land redistribution which gave nearly 2 ha. of land to every family (assuming a family size of five) might alter the social and economic organisation of the villages so drastically that it becomes difficult to be at all certain about likely output and employment effects. Nevertheless, this simulation suggests that a radical land redistribution will improve the condition of the rural poor significantly, but would do relatively little for the urban poor.

Table 4.8: Equality in Agriculture: Results of a Simulated Land Redistribution

| | Initial | | New | | |
| | Per capita incomes (Rs) | Income shares (%) | Per capita incomes (Rs) | Income shares (%) | Change in income (%) |
Income groups					
Rural					
Bottom	171.0	8.4	382.9	17.5	123.9
Middle	376.3	19.1	595.1	28.1	58.1
Top	942.3	46.4	631.1	28.9	− 33.0
Total rural personal incomes[a]	202.54	73.9	219.55	74.5	8.4
Gini coefficient		0.344		0.102	
Urban					
Bottom	234.1	2.7	261.9	2.9	11.9
Middle	540.5	6.5	580.8	6.5	7.5
Top	1442.7	16.9	1475.1	16.1	2.2
Total urban personal incomes[a]	71.87	26.1	75.14	25.5	4.6
Gini coefficient		0.363		0.348	
All-India Total personal incomes[a]	274.41	100	294.69	100	7.4
Total employment[b]	94.72		101.64		7.3
Gross output[a]	436.51		466.21		6.8

a. Measured in thousand million rupees.

b. Measured in millions of man years.

These simulation results are of a different order from those on income redistribution. Where income redistribution involved changes in the levels of the variables, changes in the shares in agricultural incomes, as from a land redistribution, involve changes in a set of important structural coefficients of the model. This change in the coefficients not only changes the agricultural distribution directly, but also alters the pattern of income flows within the model. Through their improved shares from agriculture the rural poor and middle classes now gain a significantly larger share in the entire process of income spillover,[14] thus benefiting additionally whenever the incomes of other groups rise. In this respect changing the share in incomes generated which accrues to the poor, whether through land redistribution or otherwise, makes a fundamental improvement to the position of the rural poor, bringing them this double source of sustained increase in income.[15]

Notes

1. See Chapter 3, especially Table 3.2; 2 per cent also goes to the urban areas.

2. The expenditure patterns of the various groups are described and compared in Chapter 1: see especially Tables 1.3, 1.4 and 1.5, pages 35, 37, 38. For expenditure elasticities, see Table 1.6, page 39. For the distribution of value added, see Chapter 3, especially Table 3.2, page 83.

3. The rural-urban shares in the total population are 81 per cent to 19 per cent, and in disposable income 74 per cent to 26 per cent.

4. Unless it performs a 'pump-priming' role of a type beyond the scope of our model.

5. Equivalently, because of the operation of spillovers, a maintained transfer of Rs 10 would raise the equilibrium income of the rural poor by *more* than Rs 10.

6. See Chapter 1.

7. However, for the sake of comparability we continue with the assumption that the transference of income to rural bottom comes from the rural top while the urban bottom receive their transfers from urban top.

8. It should be noted that the estimates of the income spillovers summarised in Tables 4.1 and 4.2 may no longer be accurate measures of these changes. The estimates given were evaluated at the original mean income levels of each group and, with an income change as large as 100 per cent, the implications of the non-linearity of the model become significant.

9. The assumptions of the Leontief model, within which we are working for the moment, rule out supply constraints.

10. It is well known that the land requirement for a given amount of calories obtained from animal foods is much greater than the land required to obtain the same amount of calories from plant foods. In an earlier estimate of the land requirements for a balanced diet Sinha (1961, p. 146) found that for a diet based only on plant food the land needed was around 0.41 hectares (ha.) per adult, whereas 1.03 ha. were needed for a diet containing milk products.

11. Such increases in output, income and employment result from differences in marginal propensities of consumption expenditure of various classes and *not* because of likely changes in attitudes and the resulting incentives (or disincen-

tives). We do not wish to minimise the importance of the latter, but point out that our model does not take account of any such factors. Since our model assumes perfect elasticity of supply of inputs, it cannot say anything about the constraints which might arise with such a radical redistribution. Some of these considerations are taken up in Chapter 7.

12. See United Nations ECAFE (1972, especially Tables 14-17).

13. This statement cannot easily be generalised; much would depend on the *per capita* availability of land. In most Latin American and African countries a less radical distribution might allow a much larger income to the rural population therefore would generate higher employment.

14. Accordingly, the pattern of spillovers shown in Tables 4.1 and 4.2 no longer applies.

15. We also simulated, for exploratory purposes, the changes which would follow the completely equal distribution of incomes from all production sectors, and the consequent equalising of *per capita* incomes. Total incomes increased so substantially, due to the increase in the overall marginal propensity to consume, that basic needs for all could be achieved. However, the magnitude of the institutional and structural changes involved in such a drastic redistribution make it highly doubtful whether any part of the model structure would continue to apply.

5 THE EMPLOYMENT IMPLICATIONS OF INCOME DISTRIBUTION

The ability of any group to provide for its basic needs tends to be directly and fairly closely related to its level of income. The creation of incomes for individual groups, and particularly for the poor, as we discussed it in Chapter 4, is therefore a major aspect of the attack on poverty. A related, but still rather separate aspect, in a labour-surplus economy, is the provision of employment. The availability of work is of particular importance for the poorer groups whose command over property income is at best limited and typically non-existent. But while access to work opportunities implies access to income, the creation of income and the creation of employment are not perfectly correlated. Because of the varying factor proportions used in production and the varying size distributions of the incomes generated, expenditure on different commodities may have a different impact on employment and on the generation of incomes. The creation of employment is therefore, in its own right, a policy objective of importance.

In particular, it has been suggested that more employment is generated, per unit of income, through the consumption basket of the poor than through the consumption basket of the rich (ILO, 1970). If the composition of the consumption basket of the poor, combined with the employment intensities of the various commodities, generates, at the margin, a larger volume of employment than in the case of the rich, then the opportunity exists for the redistribution of income from rich to poor to raise the total level of employment. The limited volume of subsequent work on the employment intensity of the consumer's basket at different levels of income has tended to confirm this hypothesis. But although this generalisation has been put forward, relative employment intensity is obviously an empirical matter; moreover, since Engel elasticities, technology and relative factor prices all vary between countries and over time, estimates will be specific to individual countries and dates. However, before considering the marginal employment intensity of the consumption baskets of the various groups we shall first look at the relative employment intensities of individual constituent sectors, as estimated through our model.

Sectoral Employment Intensities

The simplest measure of the relationship between output and employment in any sector is its 'employment coefficient'. This is the employment in the sector per unit of gross output, calculated by dividing the total labour force in the sector by its gross output. However, this measure, sometimes known as the 'direct' employment intensity, incorporates only that employment which is created directly within the sector itself, through the production of its own output; the impact on employment in other sectors through the purchase of intermediate inputs, and any consequent feedback to the sector itself, are excluded. It has been widely recognised for some years that, since sectors can differ considerably in the degree and range of these 'indirect effects', an adequate measure of sectoral employment implications should take account of them.[1]

The direct plus indirect effects of a unit of final output in any sector can be calculated within an open input-output framework in several simple steps: first, the inverse matrix of input-output coefficients, $(I-A)^{-1}$, is post-multiplied by a final demand vector with a unit element in the relevant (i-th) sector and zeros elsewhere; the resulting vector expresses the gross output requirements from all sectors (for the i-th sector this is identically the i-th column of the inverse matrix) associated with a unit of final demand in sector i; then, pre-multiplying the gross output (column) vector by a (row) vector of employment coefficients yields the sum of the direct and indirect employment generated in all sectors by the production of a unit of final output in the i-th sector.

This method of calculating the direct plus indirect employment effects of a unit change in final demand applies to the standard open Leontief system, where all final demand is exogenously determined. Our model, however, is a semi-closed one with endogenous personal incomes and consumption expenditure. Consequently any change in that part of final demand which is exogenous affects not only the gross output vector but also the level and distribution of personal incomes and hence the level and pattern of private consumption. In our model, therefore, the employment intensity must be redefined to be the increment of employment created in the economy per unit increment of exogenously determined final demand in any given sector.

Estimates of these employment intensities for several groups of sectors are presented in column 1 of Table 5.1, page 116. These were obtained by first increasing the final demand of every sector in the sector group by a given, small percentage, the final demand of all other sectors remaining unchanged, and then allowing the system to converge to a new equilibrium.[2] This procedure was carried out separately for each group of sectors. The employment intensity of any group is then the ratio of the resulting change in employment to the rupee value of the change in the group's final demand. The methodology for calculating the marginal employment effects is thus identical to that used in the previous chapter for calculating the effects of an income injection.

Table 5.1: Employment Intensities of Sector Groups

Sector groups	No. of persons employed per million Rs of final demand				Ratio (col. 1/ col. 3)
	Closed system	Rank	Open system	Rank	
	(1)	(2)	(3)	(4)	(5)
Agriculture (excluding animal husbandry)	1,157	2	363	3	3.2
Animal husbandry	1,062	5	247	6	4.3
Total primary[a]	1,134	I	338	I	3.4
Food products	1,006	6	288	5	3.5
Textiles and footwear	1,118	3	506	2	2.2
Wood products, etc.	1,174	1	519	1	2.3
Leather and leather products	933	7	243	7	3.8
Basic metals, metal products, etc.	623	10	173	9	3.6
Chemicals and petroleum	579	11	157	10	3.7
Other manufacturing	636	9	189	8	3.4
Total manufacturing	890	III	295	II	3.0
Construction	674	8	141	11	4.8
Transport and services	1,069	4	313	4	3.4
Total other sectors[b]	949	II	261	III	3.6

a. Total primary includes forestry, mining and plantations.
b. Includes electricity.

The ranking of the sector groups, on the basis of employment intensity, is shown in column (2), the roman numerals ranking the three major sectoral groups, primary, secondary and tertiary, and the arabic numerals the more disaggregated groups. Among the three major sectors employment created per rupee of additional final demand is greatest in the case of primary sectors[3] and lowest in the case of manufacturing;

the spread, however, is not very great, the latter figure amounting to 78 per cent of the former. The lower level of aggregation again reveals no systematic relationship between employment intensity and the primary-secondary-tertiary division; each of the three major sectors is represented within the four groups recording the highest employment intensity — wood products, agriculture, textiles and footwear, and transport and services. The disparities among the groups are now significantly wider, the employment effect of the lowest ranking sector, chemicals and petroleum, being only half that of the highest, wood and other products. With disaggregation to the full 77 sectors the variation becomes considerably wider again.

Since in a semi-closed system the indirect employment effects of an increase in final demand include effects through consumption expenditure, in addition to the more familiar ones through interindustry purchases, there is no reason to expect the employment intensities from the semi-closed system to be of the same magnitude or rank order as those which would result if the system were open. Indeed, because of the income-expenditure feedback, the intensities from the closed system will typically be larger.

In order to emphasise these differences, the employment intensities derivable by treating our model as an open system are shown in column (3) of Table 5.1, with the ranking of these intensities in column (4). On the average, the figures from the closed system are slightly more than three times the size of those from the open system (column (5)). Furthermore, the ordering of the intensities is different. Agriculture, for example, ranked third under the open system, rises to second place, displacing textiles and footwear, when the system is closed. The employment derived through consumption expenditure increases the employment intensity of agriculture by the multiple 3.2, against only 2.2 for textiles and footwear. Even at the three-sector level of aggregation changes in ranking occur, the secondary and tertiary groups reversing their positions between the closed and open versions. Furthermore, the disparities between sectors in their employment effects are considerably reduced in the closed model, the lowest sector having half of the employment potential of the highest in the closed model, against one quarter in the open model.

It can be seen from these results that the employment intensities estimated from the conventional open input-output model are at best a very limited guide to the employment potential of a sector once it is set in a closed model.[4] The levels of employment potential by sector, and the relative sectoral rankings in the semi-closed model, might well support a different set of policy conclusions.[5]

Employment Intensities of the Consumer's Basket

For present purposes, differences in sectoral employment intensities
are important for the way they interact with the expenditure patterns
of consumers at different income levels to give differences in the
volume of employment created by the marginal rupee of income. Our
estimates of the marginal employment intensity of the consumption
basket of each of our six classes, at its mean income level, are shown in
Table 5.2. Marginal employment intensity is calculated on the same
basis as the sectoral intensities, as the change in the equilibrium level of
total employment in the economy following a Re 1 injection to the
group's disposable income. Since, through spillovers, the incomes and
consumption of all groups change with the injection, the marginal
employment effect incorporates employment not only created directly
and through intermediate purchases, but also through all the additional
incomes generated by the initial injection. Thus, by being calculated
through a semi-closed model these estimates are not directly comparable with others available, all of which have been derived through open
models.

Table 5.2: Marginal Employment Intensity of Consumer's Basket, by
Class*

		Income class	
Area	Bottom	Middle	Top
Rural	0.837	0.950	0.775
Urban	0.735	0.930	0.709

*Figures are in man years per thousand rupees.

Contrary to the speculations which tend to be put forward, the
marginal employment intensity of the consumer's basket does not vary
monotonically with the level of disposable income *per capita*. The
employment created per rupee of additional income for the poor is
certainly greater than the corresponding effect for an income change
for the rich, implying that the redistribution of income from rich to
poor would result in a net increase in total employment. But, more
strikingly, the marginal effect is greater in the case of the middle
income groups, suggesting that they are the most favourable target
group from the point of view of securing the maximum impact on

employment. Moreover, a rupee of extra income given to any of the rural classes creates a larger volume of additional employment than a rupee to the corresponding class in urban areas, suggesting that a redistribution of income in favour of the rural population would again bring a net increase in total employment.

In our semi-closed model the employment effect is made up of two parts, the part attributable directly to the injection and the part attributable to the associated income changes. As the discussion in the previous chapter indicated, income spillovers are of great importance, both for their absolute size and for their pervasiveness; ultimately they affect every income group. It is correspondingly instructive to break down the increase in total employment into the parts attributable to the income change of each class separately, either injection plus spillover, or spillover only.

To do this, we use the concept of the (partial) marginal employment effect of a Re 1 change in the disposable income of a group, with the incomes of all other groups held constant to eliminate the effects through income spillovers. Estimates of these groupwise marginal employment effects were derived by multiple regression of total employment on the levels of disposable income of the six classes. The observations for the regression were generated by simulation. For each observation the income of one group was notionally increased by a given amount and the associated levels of income for all other groups and of total employment were derived from the new equilibrium. This process was repeated for each income class in turn, several observations being generated each time by income injections of varying sizes. Each of the estimated coefficients from this regression is then the (partial) marginal employment effect of one rupee of income, injection or spillover, of that group.

These marginal employment coefficients, for each class, are shown in column (1) of Table 5.3, page 120. By excluding the effects on employment of all derived income changes they are, of course, substantially smaller than the employment intensities shown in Table 5.2 The overall pattern, however, is closely similar. The highest coefficients are again those of the two middle groups, although with the rural bottom class now much closer to them. The lowest coefficients are for the urban top class, as before, and now also the urban bottom class. The correlation coefficient between the two sets is 0.959. The incorporation of income spillovers into the measurement of the employment effects of income changes, by class, thus alters the level markedly but the pattern only slightly.

Table 5.3: Employment Effect of an Increment in Income to the Rural Bottom Class*

Group	Marginal employment coefficient (1)	Income change (Rs) (2)	Employment change (1) x (2)	Per cent of total employment change
Rural				
Bottom				
Injection	0.252	1.000	0.252	30.1
Spillover	0.252	0.213	0.054	6.5
Middle	0.270	0.520	0.140	16.7
Top	0.216	1.183	0.256	30.6
All rural	0.241	2.916	0.702	83.8
Urban				
Bottom	0.199	0.065	0.013	1.6
Middle	0.255	0.161	0.041	4.9
Top	0.200	0.414	0.083	9.9
All urban	0.214	0.640	0.137	16.4
Total	0.235	3.556	0.839	100

* Employment change is measured in man years per thousand rupees.

The increase in total employment contributed by each class, following an income injection to any single class, is then estimated as the product of the marginal employment coefficient (per rupee) and the change in class income, measured in rupees. The income spillovers to result from a Re 1 injection of income to any class have already been presented and discussed (Table 4.1, page 95). The decomposition of the total employment change to result from a Re 1 income injection to the rural bottom class is given in detail in Table 5.3. Of the total employment change to result from a Re 1 income injection to this class, 0.000837 man years, only 30 per cent derives directly from the injection itself, the remaining 70 per cent coming through income spillovers. The impact on employment of the injection is fractionally exceeded, at 30.6 per cent, by the impact through income spillover to the rural rich.

The corresponding decomposition of the total employment into the proportions attributable to each class is shown in summary form in Table 5.4, page 121, where in each column the income change originates with a different class.

Several fairly clear implications emerge from this analysis of the employment effects of income changes. While employment intensities differ significantly between sectors, the effect of this through consumers' baskets is quite limited. The employment intensity of the baskets can be measured inclusive or exclusive of effects through derived income changes, but since the two are closely correlated across classes the measure adopted affects the level much more importantly than the pattern of effects.

Table 5.4: Employment Effects of Income Changes by Class

| | | Per cent of total employment change from Re 1 income injection to | | | | | |
| | | Rural | | | Urban | | |
Group	Marginal employment coefficient	Bottom	Middle	Top	Bottom	Middle	Top
Rural							
Bottom	0.252	36.6[a]	6.4	6.3	6.0	6.2	6.0
Middle	0.270	16.7	47.2[a]	19.3	17.7	19.1	18.9
Top	0.216	30.6	25.9	52.0[a]	30.2	25.2	24.0
All rural		83.8	79.4	77.6	53.9	50.5	48.9
Urban							
Bottom	0.199	1.6	1.9	2.0	28.9[a]	2.1	2.2
Middle	0.255	4.9	6.2	6.6	5.8	34.1[a]	6.9
Top	0.200	9.9	12.7	13.7	11.3	13.5	42.0[a]
All urban		16.4	20.8	22.3	46.0	49.7	51.1
Total change in employment		0.837 (100)	0.950 (100)	0.775 (100)	0.735 (100)	0.930 (100)	0.709 (100)

a. Denotes the class receiving the initial income increase.

When the derived income effects are included, much greater insight is obtained into the process of employment creation, as the income spillovers bring significant changes to the positions of the individual groups even although the eventual relative effect on employment is not greatly altered.

Employment Potential of Income Redistribution

The main conclusion which emerges from this examination of the employment intensities of the consumption baskets of the various groups in India is that the potential for employment creation through the redistribution of income seems quite limited. The employment intensity of the consumer's basket at different income levels is the outcome jointly of his consumption pattern and the sectorwise employment intensities. Suggestions such as that the consumption basket of the poor tends to create more employment per rupee because it consists predominantly in goods of simple manufacture, are essentially empirical propositions, valid only if the position of a commodity in the consumer's marginal expenditure pattern is systematically correlated with its employment intensity in production.

We have extended the concept of the employment intensity of the consumer's basket to a semi-closed model, where the change in employment to result from an income change includes the employment created directly through input purchases and through the income spillovers. Empirically however, this extension proved surprisingly uninteresting, the marginal employment effect of the consumer's basket calculated on this basis, although much greater, being very highly correlated with the conventional measurement of direct plus indirect effects.

When estimated, the marginal employment intensity of the consumer's basket proved to be non-monotonic, with the highest levels for the middle income groups. Since these intensities represent the sectoral employment effects weighted by the marginal expenditure shares at different income levels, there seems no reason to expect them necessarily to vary monotonically or even particularly smoothly between the three income levels at which we could estimate them. Hypotheses based on the assumption of systematic relationships in this area, despite their plausibility and attractive policy implications, are not empirically validated among the groups we have defined for India.

The differences observed in the employment intensities of the consumer's basket at different income levels, however, still imply that a net increase in employment could be obtained by a redistribution of income away from the classes where the effect is lowest, the top classes, to those where it is higher.[6] The partial redistribution which would make the greatest contribution to increasing employment would be one which would not be a policy choice on other grounds, from both the top and bottom classes to the middle income groups. The type of redistribution which is desirable on other grounds, income transfers to the bottom classes, has a minimal impact on employment. When the incomes of both the rural and urban poor are doubled simultaneously by transfers from the respective top classes the increase in total employment to result is 1.6 per cent.[7] Even extending the concept of redistribution to the limit, by redistributing income from the top class to the bottom until all converge within the middle income range, does not expand employment significantly. Total equality in the distribution of incomes raises employment by 14 per cent; but, as total incomes rise by 12.5 per cent as a consequence of the redistribution, the effect through the employment intensities themselves is negligible. But as we indicated earlier in relation to the structural changes in the context of a radical land redistribution, a complete equality of incomes must imply such fundamental institutional and structural changes in the economy that the results from model simulations can, at the very most, give only the most tentative indication.

Since little contribution to employment creation can be gained through income redistribution the solution to the problem of unemployment, as with other aspects of basic needs, must involve growth. It is to this area that we now turn.

Notes

1. For pioneering work in this area, see Rasmussen (1956) and Chenery and Watanabe (1958). The approach was given considerable impetus by the work of Hirschman (1958) although the concept of 'backward linkages', which he emphasised, was not set explicitly in an input-output framework. Two recent surveys are by Schultz (1976) and Stern (1977). The estimation of direct plus indirect effects for India from an open input-output system has been undertaken by Hazari and Krishnamurthy (1970), in a very compressed paper. Their measure of employment is the wage bill, not labour requirements.

2. The change in final demand was fed in through the 'other final demand' vector rather than through the endogenous private consumption vector.

3. Our stringent definition of employment in agriculture, in man years, consisting of 300 man days, should be remembered here.

4. For a comparable set of results for Korea, see Stern (1977, pp. 25-6).

5. It should also be noted that since our model is non-linear, as well as semi-closed, sectoral employment intensities are not constant but vary with the levels of output and income at which they are estimated. The estimates which we give are made at the base equilibrium levels of output and income. They thus parallel the estimates of the Engel elasticities for the non-linear expenditure functions, which are evaluated at the mean incomes of the various classes. Moreover, because of the non-linearities the employment intensities are not strictly invariant with respect to the size of the exogenous change in final demand. We have used an increment of 10 per cent throughout, as sufficiently large for minor numerical inconsistencies within the model to be unimportant even where derived output and employment changes are small, but still sufficiently small to be adequate approximations.

6. See Tables 4.4, 4.5 and 4.6, pages 101, 102, 106.

7. See Table 4.6C, page 106.

6 ECONOMIC GROWTH AND THE DISTRIBUTION OF INCOME

Simple division of the total national income of India by the population reveals that available output, perfectly equally shared out, is barely sufficient to meet the basic needs of all. Thus even the most egalitarian distribution conceptually possible scarcely secures the elimination of absolute poverty. While even in the most developed economies income transfers are a necessary part of any national policy for ensuring the provision of basic needs for all, it is clear that a fundamental attack on poverty in India must require economic growth. But a lesson of the last two decades, in India as in many developing countries, is that the process of economic growth may bring little benefit to the poor.[1] Moreover, in many countries the process of economic growth seems to be accompanied by an increase in overt unemployment.

In this chapter, therefore, we use our model to explore, by simulation, the implications of economic growth for the distribution of personal incomes, among classes and between rural and urban areas, and for the level of total employment. We will examine these topics from two aspects. First we will assess the implications for income distribution and employment of growth strategies based on alternative groups of sectors — in agriculture on foodgrains, non-food grains, and animal husbandry, in manufacturing on light industry and heavy industry, and on services. We will then focus more directly on distributional questions, simulating the implications for all other groups of income growth concentrated on one group. As an extension of this, of particular relevance for policy, we simulate the income injections which are necessary to secure a doubling of the incomes of the poor and trace their implications for sectoral outputs, the distribution of income, and employment. Finally we attempt an assessment of the implications of a hypothetical growth strategy based on current Indian experience. As with income redistribution, the key to our analysis of the distributional implications of alternative growth strategies will be the income flows or spillovers discussed in detail in Chapter 4.

Alternative Sectoral Growth Strategies

The simulation of the consequences of output growth in a target sector group begins with an (exogenous) increase in its final demand;

the production of the required gross output, both in the target sector and in its intermediate suppliers, generates additional value added, distributed among the income classes, which in turn brings further changes in the endogenous consumption element of sectoral final demand. The changes in output, incomes and employment which emerge in the new equilibrium are thus partly the direct consequence of the increase in exogenous final demand and partly derived effects from it, either through interindustry purchases or through consumers' expenditure from the additional incomes generated. Since the impact of a change in final demand on gross outputs, value added and employment in our model, due to its semi-closed nature, differs from the impact in the more familiar open models, sectorwise changes are shown, for selected groups, in Table 6.1, page 126.

The highest multiplier, both in terms of gross output and value added generated, is for animal husbandry, although both foodgrains and non-food crops (predominantly cash crops) are only marginally lower. Thus a development strategy spearheading agricultural sectors or animal husbandry will, on the basis of multipliers incorporating consumption expenditure endogenised through the income distribution, have the greatest impact on the overall level of gross output and national income. But in an agriculture-based strategy one-half of the additional output is created outside the agricultural sector, predominantly in services. Light industries, the major part of the manufacturing sector, occupy an intermediate position. Their gross output requirements from agriculture are substantial, reflecting both the use of food and fibre inputs and food purchases in consumption. Heavy industry and services, on the other hand, have relatively low multipliers in terms of both gross output and value added; in particular their impact on agriculture is only one-half of that from light industry.

As would be expected from the discussion of sectoral employment intensities above,[2] employment created per rupee of additional final demand is greatest in the case of foodgrains, followed by animal husbandry and light industries; the employment potential of services and, particularly, heavy industry is significantly lower, Re 1 of additional final demand in the case of heavy industry creating only half of the additional employment created by an additional rupee of demand for foodgrains.

Combining the output and employment effects of the various sectors, it seems clear that, within the context of our static model with no supply constraints, development strategies based on agriculture, animal husbandry and light industries will have a significantly greater impact

Table 6.1: Gross Output, Value Added and Employment Created in Major Sector Groups per Rupee Increase in Final Demand in Each Target Sector Group (Rs and percentages)*

Sector groups	Target sector group							
	Food	Non-food grains	Total agriculture	Animal husbandry	Light industries	Heavy industries	All manufacturing	Services excluding 'other services'
Agriculture	1.92 (42.1)	1.85 (41.0)	1.87 (41.2)	1.14 (23.4)	1.01 (21.4)	0.44 (11.8)	0.84 (19.0)	0.56 (14.4)
Animal husbandry	0.31 (4.8)	0.31 (6.9)	0.31 (7.0)	1.30 (26.6)	0.26 (5.6)	0.17 (4.5)	0.24 (5.4)	0.21 (5.4)
Total primary	2.27 (49.8)	2.19 (48.6)	2.23 (49.0)	2.48 (50.8)	1.35 (28.8)	0.73 (19.5)	1.17 (26.4)	0.87 (22.4)
Food products	0.25 (5.4)	0.24 (5.4)	0.24 (5.4)	0.30 (6.1)	0.79 (16.9)	0.14 (3.9)	0.61 (13.9)	0.18 (4.6)
Textiles and footwear	0.18 (3.9)	0.18 (4.0)	0.17 (3.8)	0.18 (3.7)	0.55 (11.8)	0.11 (3.0)	0.43 (9.8)	0.13 (3.5)
Metals and metal products	0.08 (1.9)	0.09 (1.9)	0.09 (1.9)	0.09 (1.8)	0.10 (2.1)	1.32 (35.3)	0.43 (9.7)	0.22 (5.6)
Total manufacturing	0.73 (16.0)	0.71 (15.7)	0.73 (16.0)	0.77 (15.8)	1.94 (41.5)	1.97 (52.7)	1.94 (43.9)	0.84 (21.6)
Total services	1.57 (34.4)	1.61 (35.7)	1.59 (35.0)	1.64 (33.6)	1.39 (29.7)	1.05 (28.1)	1.31 (29.6)	2.19 (56.3)
Total gross output	4.56 (100)	4.51 (100)	4.54 (100)	4.88 (100)	4.68 (100)	3.75 (100)	4.42 (100)	3.89 (100)
Total value added	3.43 (75.2)	3.49 (77.5)	3.45 (75.9)	3.52 (72.1)	2.88 (61.6)	2.09 (55.9)	2.67 (60.3)	2.53 (64.8)
Total employment (man days x 1,000)	1.233	0.925	1.157	1.065	0.993	0.620	0.890	0.776

*Figures in parentheses are percentages of the change in total gross output resulting from a Re 1 increase in final demand in the target sector groups.

on gross output, value added and employment than strategies in which heavy industries or services predominate.

Alternative Development Strategies and the Distribution of Incomes

Turning now to the implications of alternative development strategies for the distribution of personal incomes, Table 6.2, page 128, summarises the relative shares of the rural and urban areas and of the six income classes in personal incomes generated following a Re 1 increase in final demand in one of the various target sectors.[3]

The increases in total personal incomes from the various sectoral strategies closely parallel those in gross output and value added. The agricultural sectors and animal husbandry have the greatest multiplier effects on personal incomes, followed, at some distance, by light industries, while services and, particularly, heavy industry have significantly lower figures. One rupee of additional final demand for heavy industry creates just over half of the personal incomes generated by Re 1 of additional demand for animal husbandry.

With every sectoral strategy the rural areas receive between 55 and 77 per cent of the personal incomes generated; thus the major part of the incomes created, on any sectoral strategy, even heavy industry, flow to the rural areas. However, since the rural areas contain 81 per cent of the national population and receive 74 per cent of existing personal incomes these major shares are barely sufficient to maintain their relative position *vis-à-vis* the urban areas. In agriculture-based strategies spearheading food or non-food grains or animal husbandry, the rural share in incomes generated just exceeds their current share in total income and falls slightly short of their share in population. Thus in terms of the distribution of incomes between rural and urban areas, even agriculture-based strategies barely favour the rural areas. In the case of light industries, services and, particularly, heavy industry the urban bias in personal incomes generated is quite pronounced. There is thus no sectoral development strategy which favours the rural areas; at best strategies based on agriculture will not disadvantage them.

For the rural poor the situation is much bleaker even than this. Only from the expansion of foodgrains do they gain a share in personal incomes greater than their current income share. From all other sectors, including non-food grains, animal husbandry and light industries and services in addition to the expected heavy industries, they receive a share in marginal income below their, already low, current share.

In common with the general urban bias in the pattern of incomes generated the situation for the urban poor is rather more encouraging.

Table 6.2: Percentage Distribution of Incremental Incomes from Alternative Sectoral Development Strategies

Income groups	Initial shares	Foodgrains	Non-food grains	Total agricul-ture	Animal husban-dry	Light indus-tries	Heavy indus-tries	Total manufacturing	Services other than 'other services'
Rural									
Bottom	8.41	9.88	7.14	9.25	6.82	7.77	6.12	7.31	6.92
Middle	19.07	20.35	19.71	20.23	23.86	20.85	18.87	20.38	21.03
Top	46.34	46.22	49.14	46.53	45.17	39.22	30.10	37.31	34.35
Total rural	73.81	76.45	75.99	76.01	75.85	67.84	55.09	65.00	62.30
Urban									
Bottom	2.74	2.33	2.29	2.31	2.27	3.18	4.08	3.46	4.26
Middle	6.53	5.81	6.01	6.07	5.97	7.77	10.71	8.46	10.14
Top	16.92	15.41	15.71	15.61	15.91	21.21	30.10	23.08	23.30
Total urban	26.19	23.55	24.00	23.99	24.15	32.16	44.89	35.00	37.70
All-India	100	100	100	100	100	100	100	100	100
Total personal income multiplier (no.)	—	3.44	3.51	3.46	3.53	2.83	1.96	2.60	2.44

Heavy industry, services and light industry all give them a marginal income share above their current level, although they do less well from the agriculture-based sectors.

In spite of their large absolute share in incomes, particularly from the agricultural sectors, the rural top class lose, in terms of their relative position, from all strategies except cash crops and even there the improvement they gain is quite small. In terms of income share even an agriculture-based strategy is only marginally in the interests of the rural rich. On the other hand, all strategies involving industries or services clearly favour all the urban classes. This relative urban bias is most pronounced in the case of the top class in the urban areas and in heavy industry.

Thus the combination of sector-wise expenditure elasticities and group shares in value added found in the base data suggests distinctly pessimistic conclusions on the impact of growth on income distribution and the incidence of poverty. The general tendency to adverse conclusions is more striking than the detailed differences between development strategies based on alternative sectoral groups. The rural population, who are by far the majority, can barely retain their existing income share, which already places them at a disadvantage, on a *per capita* basis, relative to the urban population; they scarcely gain from agriculture-based development and lose significantly from any other development strategy. Every development pattern, except one based on foodgrains, is to the disadvantage of the country's poorest group, the bottom income class in the rural areas. Every strategy based on industry or services has a strong urban bias and, while all the groups benefit, the gain to the top urban class is conspicuously large.

It is therefore obvious that the process of economic growth is likely, in general, to have adverse effects on the distribution of incomes and particularly on the relative position of the rural poor. Even a development strategy based on sectors with, as far as possible, favourable distributional implications for the various target groups, would be a relatively blunt instrument for influencing the distribution of incomes even if its implications for the structure of output were acceptable. We therefore turn now to consider the distributional aspects of economic growth, focusing not on the pattern of output growth by sector but on the growth of incomes by income class.

Growth Directed to Income Classes

A growth strategy with a strong focus on distribution could be formulated in terms of implementing policies which secure a given injection of income to target groups. Through the expenditure patterns of the income recipients the injection itself will have further implications for the distribution of incomes. It is these implications which we will explore, abstracting from the sectoral implications of the measures used to achieve the income injection. Thus if, for example, new incomes are created for the rural poor by employing them on rural construction projects, the need for purchased inputs is assumed away in order to sharpen the focus on the derived effects on incomes. The distribution of personal incomes, between rural and urban areas and among the income classes, to result per rupee of income created for each group is shown in Table 6.3.

Table 6.3: Percentage Distribution of Incremental Incomes from Income Growth by Class

| | | Income growth for | | | | | |
| | | Rural | | | Urban | | |
Income groups	Initial share	Bottom	Middle	Top	Bottom	Middle	Top
Rural							
Bottom	8.41	34.1	6.1	5.6	5.2	5.8	5.3
Middle	19.07	14.6	41.9	16.2	14.5	16.7	15.4
Top	46.34	33.3	28.8	54.5	30.8	27.5	24.5
Total rural	73.81	82.0	76.8	76.3	50.5	50.0	45.2
Urban							
Bottom	2.74	1.7	2.2	2.3	32.0	2.4	2.4
Middle	6.53	4.5	5.8	5.9	5.0	31.6	6.0
Top	16.92	11.6	15.2	15.5	12.4	15.9	46.4
Total urban	26.19	18.0	23.2	23.7	49.5	50.0	54.8
All-India	100	100	100	100	100	100	100
Total personal income multiplier	—	3.56	3.96	3.42	3.34	3.94	3.2

The largest personal income multipliers are associated with income injections to the middle classes in both rural and urban areas; this is, of course, consistent with our findings on spillover effects and on employment creation.[4] When a new, higher level of income is generated for one of the rural groups more than three-quarters of the resultant overall increase remains in the rural areas. Income growth for any of the rural groups thus improves the rural share in total personal incomes, an effect which is particularly pronounced in the case of income growth for the rural poor. With income growth for the urban groups, on the other hand, half of the resultant increase remains in the urban areas, giving them a share in the incremental income almost double their existing share. Thus, as is not unexpected in the light of our earlier discussion of income spillovers, income growth directed to individual groups does produce a rural or urban bias in the resulting distribution, but with the urban bias from growth for the urban groups significantly more pronounced than the rural bias in the case of rural growth. Direct increases in income for rural and urban groups replicate, in accentuated form, the pattern of rural-urban income distribution associated in the one case with agricultural development and in the other with the growth of industry and services.

The target groups themselves retain a share between 31 and 55 per cent of the total increase in incomes to result from the injection. The share retained by the rural and urban poor and by the urban middle class is significantly lower than that by the other three classes, particularly the rural top class. The approximate comparability of these shares, against the 81/19 rural-urban distribution of population, re-emphasises the urban bias in the income flows. Only income creation directly for the rural or urban poor yields any improvement in their income share.

Doubling the Incomes of the Poor

The simultaneous doubling of the incomes of both the rural and urban poor through growth in terms of income injections to them exclusively represents an extreme configuration of a redistribution-through-growth strategy, but one with strong policy appeal in terms of the attack on poverty. We have therefore simulated this strategy through our model to explore its implications for outputs and employment in total and by sector, for the incomes of the various groups and for the overall distribution of incomes.

Table 6.4, page 132, shows the necessary increase in total gross output and national income to be 20 per cent, and the change in employment of the same magnitude. The sectors from which the largest increases in output would be required are services (partly reflecting the semi-residual category 'other services') and animal husbandry, while increases of between 16 and 19 per cent would be required in agriculture, food products, and textiles and footwear. Thus if all growth were to be concentrated on raising the incomes of the poorest groups a substantial contribution to the reduction in poverty could be achieved from an increase in national income of 20 per cent.

Table 6.5, page 133, shows the income changes which result from doubling the incomes of the poor. Because of our assumption of an income injection where the form or sector for the income creation is unspecified, the growth of personal income exceeds the growth of output. Although, because of the much greater extent of their poverty problem, the rural areas receive three-quarters of the total injection, rural and urban incomes grow approximately in step, but with the increase in urban incomes slightly greater. Thus the urban bias in the income spillovers more than offsets the concentration of the attack on poverty into the rural areas. All the other classes also benefit substantially from the income growth of the poor, the rural rich rather less than the 24 per cent gained by the others. In terms of income shares the two bottom classes, as intended, improve their positions considerably, with the rural rich the group at whose expense the gains are predominantly made.

Table 6.4: Doubling the Incomes of the Poor through Economic Growth: Output and Employment Changes

Sector	Gross output[a]		Value added[a]		Employment[b]	
	Initial level	Percentage change	Initial level	Percentage change	Initial level	Percentage change
Agriculture	142.4	16.6	117.2	16.7	45.7	15.1
Animal husbandry	27.3	28.0	16.6	28.0	2.8	27.9
Total primary	178.3	18.0	141.4	17.7	49.7	15.7
Food products	37.2	20.4	10.8	18.7	3.7	10.4
Textiles and footwear	25.5	17.1	6.1	17.1	5.7	14.6
Metals and metal products	32.1	5.9	10.3	5.8	2.4	5.4
Total manufacturing	127.0	14.8	37.5	13.9	16.5	12.3
Total services	131.2	25.3	98.0	31.2	28.5	33.5
Total - all sectors	436.5	19.3	277.0	21.9	94.7	20.5

a. Gross output and value added are measured in thousand million rupees.
b. Employment is in million man years.

Doubling the incomes of the poor through the concentration of growth exclusively on them thus brings, through the operation of income spillovers, significant benefits to the other income groups, while its requirements in terms of additional output, either in total or by sector, are not particularly formidable. The broad lines of our conclusions on the net costs of redistribution through growth, therefore, largely confirm those from the earlier analysis of redistribution through income transfer.

Table 6.5: Doubling the Incomes of the Poor through Economic Growth: Income Changes

Income group	Average *per capita* income (Rs) Initial	Final	Income share (%) Initial	Final	Income change (%)
Rural					
Bottom	171.0	341.9	8.4	12.9	100
Middle	376.3	469.4	19.1	18.2	24.7
Top	942.3	1128.4	46.3	42.4	19.7
All rural	495.3	644.8	73.8	73.5	30.2
Gini coefficient			0.344	0.270	
Urban					
Bottom	234.1	468.2	2.7	4.2	100
Middle	540.5	673.3	6.5	6.2	24.6
Top	1442.7	1796.1	16.9	16.1	24.5
All urban	737.1	976.1	26.1	26.5	32.4
Gini coefficient			0.363	0.301	
All-India	541.9	708.6	100	100	30.8

National Growth, Poverty and Income Distribution

As a final set of simulations of the implications of growth for income distribution and the provision of basic needs we have traced, in the context of our model, the effects on *per capita* incomes and on income shares of raising national income to a level 50 per cent above its base level. The levels of sectoral output consistent with this are taken from the detailed projections prepared in connection with the Indian Fifth Plan, their 66 sectors being matched into our 77 sector classification.[5] The growth in incomes by class and the corresponding changes in the distribution of incomes are shown in Table 6.6, page 134.

Total personal incomes increase virtually in step with national income, but urban incomes gain substantially more than rural incomes; with national income rising to 50 per cent above its base level on the postulated sectoral growth pattern, rural incomes rise by 44 per cent but urban incomes by 62 per cent. The simulation of a 'realistic' growth pattern through our model reveals very clearly the urban bias implied in the process of income generation and distribution as we have modelled it.

As national income rises by 50 per cent no group receives an income increase of less than 40 per cent, and to that extent the growth process benefits all groups significantly. However, from the point of view of distributional objectives and the provision of basic needs the picture is much less satisfactory. The group with the lowest income growth of all are the rural poor, and their already low share in total income declines further. The urban bottom class fare significantly better in terms of income growth but their increase in income is only marginally greater than that of the urban middle class and below that of the urban top class. Thus, in spite of the substantial overall improvement in levels, the distribution within both rural and urban areas deteriorates, in addition to the relative deterioration suffered by the rural areas as a whole.

Table 6.6: National Growth and Income Distribution: Results of a 50 per cent Increase in National Income

	Average *per capita* income (Rs)		Income Share (%)		Income change (%)
Income group	Initial	Final	Initial	Final	
Rural					
Bottom	171.0	241.3	8.4	8.0	41.1
Middle	376.3	551.9	19.1	18.8	46.6
Top	942.3	1347.9	46.3	44.6	43.0
All rural	495.3	712.1	73.8	71.4	43.8
Gini coefficient			0.344	0.344	
Urban					
Bottom	234.1	372.8	2.7	2.9	59.3
Middle	540.5	854.6	6.5	7.0	58.1
Top	1442.7	2360.3	16.9	18.6	63.6
All urban	737.1	1192.5	26.1	28.5	61.8
Gini coefficient			0.363	0.369	
All-India	541.9	804.6	100	100	48.5
Total employment (millions)	94.72	137.64			45.3

The bleakness of these implications for the position of the rural poor is confirmed when their average income level, after the 50 per cent increase in national income, is compared with the minimum necessary to meet basic needs. Even with no allowance for population growth in the period during which the increase in national income is being achieved, they remain significantly below the poverty line, however austerely defined. The urban poor, on the other hand, are rather better placed, the growth itself, combined with the urban bias in income spillovers, raising them more quickly towards a bare sufficiency in terms of basic needs.

The harsh conclusion thus emerges that, within the process of income generation and distribution as we have modelled it, the rural and urban poor are both relatively disadvantaged in terms of their evolving share in the incomes of their respective areas.[6] But as a consequence of the urban bias in the pattern of incomes generated, the relative disadvantage suffered by the rural poor is particularly pronounced. Even with very substantial national growth, and with no allowance for population increase, the incomes available to the rural poor will be quite inadequate, on the given distributional pattern, to provide for their basic needs.

Notes

1. For some of the leading evidence and viewpoints on this, see Myrdal (1968), Adelman and Morris (1973) and Chenery *et al*. (1974).

2. See Chapter 5, especially Table 5.1, page 116.

3. As with the changes in output and employment discussed above, the increment to personal incomes from a Re 1 increase in final demand in any sector is not, of course, its own immediate distribution to personal incomes from its value added but the increase resulting from all the derived changes in sectoral outputs and expenditure patterns.

4. See Tables 4.1, page 95, 5.2 and 5.4, pages 118, 121.

5. See Government of India Planning Commission (1973, Annexure III-1 and IV-1).

6. Our model does not incorporate technical progress. This conclusion must, therefore, be appraised in the context of the numerous findings that the rural poor have gained little as a result of Green Revolution technology. See Griffin (1971, 1975) and Dasgupta (1977).

7 THE PROJECT RESULTS AND SOME POLICY ISSUES

The model which we have been reporting on throughout this study was conceived and designed essentially as a research tool, to explore various aspects of the inter-relationships among income distribution, basic needs and employment. The first context, therefore, in which an assessment of it must be given is methodological. The model structure must be appraised: to assess the extent to which the innovations we have introduced and the particular features we have sought to develop have contributed to the range and quality of the results gained; to assess the extent to which the applicability and usefulness of the results is limited by the assumptions which have been adopted; and to indicate the directions in which further developments seem most likely to be fruitful.

While conclusions on methodological issues are of fundamental importance for analysis on which effective policy making must ultimately be based, the enormity of the human problem for India and the pressing importance, internationally, of the issues central to this study prompt more immediate and practical concern with policy issues. In conclusion, therefore, we appraise, in the light of the results from the model simulations, the likely future prospects for income distribution and the position of the poor in India, in the context of the policies currently being implemented and the contemporary debates on policy issues in India.

Income Implications Summarised

To set the scene for the appraisal both of the model itself and its implications for policy issues it will be useful to draw together the various results presented in the earlier chapters (4 to 6). The major innovation introduced in this study, and the one from which all the conclusions on the distribution of incomes ultimately derive, is the distribution among the various classes of the value added from each sector. The analysis of these distributions themselves, even outside the overall macro-model, yields a number of striking insights.[1] At the sectoral level the income shares created for the various groups are always heavily skewed against the lower income classes; while in some sectors the structure is slightly less unfavourable than in others, every

136

sectoral pattern of output gives a lower share in income created to the poor than to the higher income groups. Consequently, no rearrangement of the pattern of expenditure can bring a significant improvement in the relative position of the poor. Not quite tautologically, the poor are poor because of their consistently low share primarily in the ownership of assets and therefore incomes generated. If the incomes of the poor are to be increased this must be either through income transfer, or through growth, or through a change in the distribution of incomes created at the sectoral level.

A further implication of the low share for the poor in incomes generated is that any income transfer can bring them little, if any, sustained benefit. As soon as it is spent the major part of the resulting incomes accrues to other groups, particularly the rural top, with the poor gaining only a small share. A once-for-all transfer of income to the poor can raise their incomes only temporarily.[2] If the increase in incomes is to be maintained, within the structure as we have modelled it, the income transfer must correspondingly be placed on a permanent basis.

Sustained income transfers, even pitched at the level necessary for a significant attack on poverty, are less formidable than might be thought, in their implications both for the increased output required and for the classes from whom the transfer is made. When we simulated the doubling of the incomes of the poorest third of the population, through income transfer, the required increase in national income was only 2 per cent; even in the sectors where the changes are most heavily concentrated, agricultural products, in particular foodgrains, the necessary increase in output is rather less than 10 per cent.[3] There are two reasons for this low figure. The poorest groups, and as we have defined them they comprise 167 million people, exist at such a low level of consumption that even a doubling of their incomes does not imply a large absolute increase in demand. Moreover, many households in the top income classes are themselves at income levels at which food is still the largest single item in their marginal expenditure pattern, and the reduction in their purchases is a significant offset to the additional demand from the poor.[4]

Moreover, doubling the incomes of the poor by transfers from the rural top class to the rural poor, and from the urban top class to the urban poor, implies, in the first instance, income reductions for these groups of 18 per cent and 16 per cent respectively.[5] However, the increase in total consumption expenditure and, to some extent, the change in its sectoral pattern, in turn generates a return flow of income to the top classes, through their substantial shares in sectoral value added.

This return flow of income amounts, in total, to 31 per cent of the initial value of the transfer in the rural case. However, there is no such net return in the case of urban top. Over all, the real cost of the transfers to the top classes, in terms of the eventual reduction in their disposable incomes, comes to only 15 per cent.

While doubling the incomes of the poorest groups by income transfers would represent a significant contribution towards the provision of basic needs for all, the lower income levels of the great majority of the population make it obvious that only a limited reduction in poverty can be achieved through redistribution alone. More substantial progress towards this objective must depend on growth.

Our simulations of the impact of growth on the distribution of incomes, however, do not suggest an encouraging prospect for the position of the poor. Through the process of income spillover, the poor, like every other class, ultimately derive some share in the incomes created through growth. Every growth pattern brings them some real gain. However, the share accruing to them is typically small, and against it in any practical context must be set the growth of population and any other simultaneous changes, favourable or adverse, affecting the group's real *per capita* income. Thus in many conceivable situations their share in the incomes generated by growth may not be sufficient to ensure any reduction in poverty, even in absolute terms.

Turning from the absolute to the relative position of the poor, in terms of their shares in total incomes, our conclusions are again that, while the situation is not entirely without its hopeful aspects, the overall outlook is not encouraging. In general, the prospects for the 32 million or so urban poor are rather brighter than for the more numerous (by four times) rural poor.

Our explorations into the process of income spillover yield striking findings on the income flows between rural and urban areas. The rural areas typically receive the major part of the incomes generated following any change. When the development strategy gives priority to increases in agricultural output or rural incomes, between 70 and 80 per cent of the resulting total incomes remain in the rural areas. Even when growth is based on income injections to the urban groups or on the development of heavy industry, which is predominantly urban in location, around one-half of the incomes generated in the income-expenditure sequence flow to the rural areas.[6]

However, when these flows are adjusted to a *per capita* basis a pronounced urban bias emerges. For each rupee of additional income received by any class, rural or urban, the ultimate increase in *per capita* income in rural areas is only between 46 and 70 per cent of that received in urban areas.[7] Because of this, even a growth strategy which directs its initial impact to the rural areas, as agriculture preeminently does, yields only a marginal improvement in the income shares of the rural areas and particularly of the rural poor. At the other extreme, the development of heavy industry results in a distribution which is urban-biased on both counts, the share of the rural poor in total incomes falling by over one-quarter, from 8.4 to 6.1 per cent. Development strategies spearheaded by light industries or services, where the initial impact is divided between the rural and urban areas, bring a similar, but less marked, deterioration in the position of the rural poor and relative improvement for the urban poor.

There is, therefore, no major group of sectors whose growth improves the relative income shares of the rural and urban poor simultaneously. Growth in any group of sectors implies an adverse change for one, if not both, of these target groups. By extension, any growth strategy including a variety of these elements will have a net effect at best marginally to the advantage of one of the groups. Less contrived (or more realistic) growth strategies, such as plan projections would yield, seem likely to give a slight improvement for the urban poor, accompanied by a deterioration for the rural poor.[8]

The only policy we simulated which produced a sustained and substantial improvement in the position of the poorer groups, in rural areas only, was a change in the income shares derived from agriculture, as would follow from a land redistribution.[9] This benefited the rural poor both directly and through an enhanced share in all income spill-overs. While our treatment could be only tentative, these results strongly suggest that a change in the shares gained by the various classes in incomes generated, by means of a redistribution of land or other productive assets, or otherwise, will make a major and pervasive impact on poverty and the distribution of incomes. The magnitude of the structural changes required to produce these significant effects should not, however, be underestimated.

Some Conclusions on Model Structure

All these findings drawn from simulations with the model are, of course, conditional on the appropriateness of its structure as well as on the quality of the data used in estimation. We turn now to the appraisal of our model, seeking to identify those features which have made a positive contribution to the results gained and those features which restrict their applicability.

The major innovation introduced in our model has been to 'close the loop' of the circular flow of income by the derivation of the income distribution from value added in the individual production sectors. The major set of explorations which this has made possible has been into the full structure of income flows, across classes and between rural and urban areas. These explorations reveal that the process of income spill-over between groups is both pervasive and complex, and that the overall effect is unlikely to be adequately summarised or predicted from one or two of the leading immediate effects. Generalisations such as that the predominance of food purchases in the expenditure of the urban poor ensures the return of incomes to the rural areas, or that the purchase of services by the rich creates incomes for the poor, even while accurate in themselves, take into account such a small part of the process of income creation that they are liable to be quite misleading as to the ultimate effects.

Thus the most important conclusion which we draw is that adequate treatment of the distributional implications of alternative developments or policies requires a model which explicitly incorporates the generation of the income distribution, as well as its consequences. The closing of the loop, through a model which is at least semi-closed through the endogenous treatment of consumption, is essential. This conclusion seems to us of fundamental significance, not only for the methodology of research into income distribution and the economic status of the poor but also, at one remove, for policy making. To devise effective policies on income distribution and the provision of basic needs involves, as a prerequisite, adequate analysis of the structure of income flows. This conclusion seems almost self-evident, and yet, in spite of the prominence which has been given, over the past decade, to basic needs and the improvement of the position of the poorest groups within the income distribution, both in India and elsewhere, no comparable model, even of more limited scope, has been constructed for India, and perhaps only two or three for other countries.

In a semi-closed model with the structure we have adopted, where consumption is the only part of final demand to be treated endogenously, the distribution of incomes results from the interaction between the distribution of sectoral value added among the various income classes and their marginal expenditure patterns. In order to allow as much precision as was feasible in incorporating the detail of sectorwise income shares and groupwise expenditure patterns, we adopted the most disaggregated commodity classification consistent with the available data. In particular, we extended the disaggregation of agricultural products and services substantially beyond the classification used, for example, in the Fifth Plan model by the Indian Planning Commission.[10] This disaggregation has contributed importantly to the modelling of the income flows. The agricultural sectors are the major source of income in rural areas and particularly for the rural poor, while services play a similar, though lesser, role for the urban poor; and both food products and services are important in marginal expenditure patterns at different income levels, this importance varying strongly with income. The majority of the sectors in our classification were, however, in manufacturing industry, and played only a very minor role either in incomes generated or in marginal consumption patterns. On the evidence from our work, the view being expressed at the time our model was designed, i.e. that systematic and important relationships between the distribution of income and the level of employment might be being obscured by inadequate sectoral disaggregation, contained an element of truth. Substantial disaggregation of agricultural products and services, more substantial than is often found in official statistics, contributes to the effective modelling of income flows. The proliferation of small sectors in manufacturing industry, on the other hand, does not; thus, much of the disaggregation typically found in planning models is unnecessary for the modelling of the distribution of incomes.

The other respect in which we have sought to model the role of income distribution with precision is in allowing the expenditure functions for the individual commodities to take non-linear forms where this seemed empirically appropriate. Our prior preference for the flexibility which non-linear forms imply, with the marginal propensity to consume and the income elasticity of demand both free to vary with income, has been substantially confirmed by the non-linearity of the functional forms adopted for many commodities. Since this is the only point in our model at which non-linearity features, we can offer only a few limited comments on the role which it has played and in no way a full appraisal of its implications. The price paid for the flexibility just discussed, in effect the endogenising of some structural parameters, is in part conceptual and in part practical. Constant parameters measuring the impact of one variable on another have to be replaced by estimates specific to the levels of these, and possibly other, variables at which the evaluation is made. Thus, our estimates of parameters such as expenditure elasticities and employment intensities have typically been quoted for values of group mean incomes and other variables at their base levels. The expenditure elasticities are, as must be expected, the parameters which show the greater variability with income levels. Beyond this, the limited degree of non-linearity which we have incorporated brings noticeable, but not substantial, changes in estimates evaluated at different points. The solution procedures for a non-linear system are computationally much more laborious than for a linear system and consequently more demanding of computer resources. The difficulty which this entails, however, can easily be exaggerated. In our own case the initial version of the model solution programme was written and the early simulation runs made, without difficulty, in Delhi.

Thus the special features which we have incorporated into our model have made significant contributions to the strength and usefulness of the results. Major limitations are, however, implied by the assumptions of the standard Leontief-type framework which we have adopted. Two of these assumptions are of particular importance in the present context: the fixity of the structural coefficients and the perfect elasticity of supply of output.

The restrictiveness in principle of the assumption of the fixity of the production coefficients in an input-output system is well known, and its practical importance, relative to changes in the composition of sectoral output, relative input prices and technology, has often been assessed. We have little to add to that discussion. We have, however, extended the fixed-coefficient assumption to two further areas, employment and, more importantly, the distribution of sectoral value added among the socio-economic classes. In the latter case the assumption of fixed coefficients brings the implication that the distributional shares in any increment to sectoral value added must be identical to the average shares, an assumption which we have no evidence to support or refute. In deriving the average shares of the income classes in value added by sector we were already breaking new ground. To have estimated additionally a marginal distribution was totally outwith both our capacity and the data available. It must be conceded, however, that the assumption that marginal income shares simply replicate the average shares will certainly contribute some inertia to the distribution of incomes as it emerges from the simulations. But while our results will be biased in the direction of maintaining the existing distribution, it is impossible to indicate, without information on the relationship between the marginal and average distributions, whether this will lead to excessively optimistic or pessimistic conclusions.

As long as surplus labour in all categories remains a dominant characteristic of the Indian situation it may well be that no substantial changes will take place, although the evidence from a number of other developing countries of increasing 'dualism' in labour markets suggests that the prospects for the poor may be even bleaker than we have suggested. The distribution of value added among the income classes, in particular at the margin, seems an area in which further work, perhaps involving special surveys, could significantly strengthen the basis of the estimates.

As with all Leontief-type models, ours is most appropriately regarded as articulating only the demand side of the macro-economic processes of production and income distribution, and determining actual levels of outputs and incomes only on the very stringent assumption of perfectly elastic supply of all outputs and all factor inputs. Even its representation purely in demand terms, however, implies consistency requirements in respect of the derived demand for increases in capital stock. It is unlikely that in not formally incorporating these we have introduced any serious violation of consistency, since changes in output requirements implied by the various strategies which we have simulated are typically either within the range of existing excess capacity, as suggested by Indian commentators, or substantially less than the growth targets proposed in the various Plans.

But even where significant increases in capital stock are not necessary, replacement investment imposes a consistency requirement in respect of the volume of savings, while the marked differences in marginal savings propensities between the income classes suggest that particularly the more extreme redistribution strategies could involve inadequate levels of personal saving. Detailed simulation, however, revealed that while redistribution alone has a significant adverse effect, the impact of growth is strongly favourable, suggesting that only in the case of a major redistribution of income unaccompanied by growth might personal savings be a constraint. In the base configuration personal savings are 4.2 per cent of disposable personal incomes; doubling the incomes of both the rural and the urban poor simultaneously, by income transfer from the respective top classes, cuts this by more than half to 1.7 per cent. On the other hand virtually all growth paths, with their falling income share for the poor, have favourable savings implications, while in the strategy of redistribution-through-growth where income injections are created which double the incomes of the poor, the strong income spillover to the higher income groups raises the personal savings ratio to 10 per cent. Although an aggregate savings constraint seems unlikely in the situations we have simulated, this does not preclude specific shortages if individual savings flows are sharply reduced in a highly segmented capital market.[11]

If the use of the model is to be extended to the determination of

actual levels of outputs and incomes without the assumption of perfectly elastic supply, then the specification of supply functions and the
incorporation of prices and market-clearing conditions becomes essential. When the supply of output is assumed to depend positively on
price, any increase in demand will involve both an increase in output,
with implications for production, incomes and expenditure as we have
modelled them, and an increase in the price of the output. This increase
in price will itself affect the level and pattern of expenditure and, more
particularly, the distribution of incomes. The effects of price changes
on the income distribution could be markedly different in incidence
from the effects of quantity changes as we have been exploring them.

The development of models incorporating the effects on income
distribution through product and, by extension, factor prices is the
current major challenge in this area, involving formidable conceptual
problems even more importantly than limitations of data.[12]

The Policy Problem

Our analysis and simulation results all confirm that the key to the low
income status of the poor is the invariably low share accruing to them
from incomes generated. This is the heart of the policy problem. Since
the poor gain only a low share in value added from all sectors, manipu-
lation of the structure of output, whether through income redistribution, fiscal measures or otherwise, can bring, at best, only a marginal
improvement in their relative position. Similarly, while these distributional shares persist, the distributional aspects of the choice between
one sectoral growth strategy and another involve, at best, the choice of
which group of the poor is to receive a marginal improvement in its
relative position while the other suffers a deterioration.

The implication is inescapable that the low incomes of the poor can
be significantly increased only by direct measures. While a radical
redistribution of the existing flows of income may provide the poor
with the bare minimum for survival, it goes nowhere near meeting basic
needs on any satisfactory level. It is, therefore, only through growth
coupled with redistribution in favour of the poor that the conditions of
the poor can be improved.

Conceptually, the simplest mechanism through which redistribution
can be achieved is income transfers and the model simulations showed
that these must be continuous. Otherwise the shares of the income
classes in value added must be altered in favour of the poor. The basic
reasons for the low income shares of the poor lie in aspects which we
could not formally model in any detail — their weak integration into

the process of creation of factor incomes, and their low levels of owner-ship of productive assets, land, other physical capital and human capital. To improve this situation requires their greater integration into the income-creation process and the vesting of assets specifically in them, either through the creation of new assets or through the redistribution of existing ones. Until changes of this order take place income transfers and income injections can be merely palliatives, effective only as long as they are consistently renewed.

Generating adequate provision for basic needs thus comprises a two-stage problem. The fundamental solution, the creation of income-earning opportunities for the poor, while it requires immediate action, can yield significant effects only in the longer run. In the meantime emphasis must be placed on consumption transfers, particularly of foodgrains. While this may derive a partial justification from its implica-tions for labour productivity, the dominant justification can only be the social or humanitarian one of ensuring subsistence to many people whose survival, without such policies, would be in doubt.

Some Current Policies – Feeding Programmes

A number of the more obvious policies suggested by this diagnosis are already being implemented in India.[13] The two most important pro-grammes of consumption transfers are the subsidised sale of food, and school feeding programmes. In the former the state arranges to distrib-ute foodgrains, on a ration basis, at subsidised prices through 'fair price' shops. Such programmes cover mainly urban areas but in Kerala they are extended to rural areas as well. According to a recent assess-ment of the Kerala programme, the poorest 30 per cent of the state's population were receiving around 1,100 calories, two-thirds of their present consumption and roughly one-half of their daily requirements, through this arrangement (UN Department of Social and Economic Affairs, 1975, pp. 43-5).

A number of Indian states operate school feeding programmes, a tradition which goes back to 1929 when Madura (now Tamil Nadu) initiated such a programme. By 1970 some 17 million people, 92 per cent of them children, were benefiting through institutional feeding programmes, and the programmes have been further extended to other vulnerable groups, such as pre-school children and pregnant women. The Planning Commission targets for these programmes are for the provision of (largely cooked) food providing around 400 calories and 15 grammes of protein per day for children attending school, covering between 100 and 200 days per year, with rather higher provision for mothers and lower for pre-school children (Government of India Planning Commission, 1973a, pp. 244-5).[14]

The immediate objective of these programmes is to improve nutritional standards, but to the extent that they also imply increased production of foodgrains they can bring a double benefit to the poor. As we showed above, agriculture is not only the principal source of income for the rural poor, but it is the sector where their relative income share is highest; and perhaps most significantly of all, a development strategy directed to foodgrain production is, in our analysis, the only growth path which brings an improvement in the relative position of the rural poor. In this way feeding programmes, although directed in the first instance at consumption levels, may also improve the income position of the poor, while in the longer run improved levels of nutrition represent an investment in higher labour productivity.[15]

Our simulations have strongly suggested that a major contribution to meeting basic needs, in terms of doubling the incomes of the poor, would not require massive increases in output. Estimates based on alternative methodologies similarly suggest that a major reduction in the incidence of malnutrition through feeding programmes is by no means unfeasible. According to FAO nearly 175 million people were receiving less than 1.2 BMR or around 1,486 calories. To raise this to around 2,000 calories, with the additional stipulation that this be provided 365 days a year, implies an annual grain requirement not exceeding 10 million tons, or around 8 per cent of current grain output. The orders of magnitude in this estimate can be confirmed in an alternative way. The Tamil Nadu Nutrition Survey (USAID, 1975, vol. II, Section D) estimated the average cost of a nutrition programme to supply 500 calories at around Re 0.24-0.28 per day (at 1971-2 prices), or between Rs 90 and 100 per person for 365 days. For a total undernourished population of 175 million this represented a total outlay equivalent to 4 per cent of GDP.

The key to the success of such programmes is efficient implementation, involving effective procurement, storage and distribution. Since the objective is the redistribution of consumption (or income) some resistance is to be expected from those from whom the procurement is made. Alternatively, at least part of the grain requirements could be met through imports, either under international food-aid programmes or through trade, but in this case any potential income benefits to the poor are lost.[16] On the administrative side, the proliferation of individual programmes – in Tamil Nadu alone there are nine separate institutional feeding programmes – strongly suggest deficiencies in co-ordination and coverage and excessive administrative machinery.[17]

The Minimum Needs Programme, introduced originally in the Fifth Five Year Plan and now expanded in the draft Sixth Plan, promotes the concept of an integrated welfare programme to improve the position of the poor in respect not only of nutrition but of drinking water supplies, sanitation and health, education, housing and electricity. The adoption of this integrated approach incorporates the recognition of the inter-relatedness of the various requirements for subsistence, where the effectiveness of a global programme will be greater than of its parts individually.

Programmes of Income and Employment Creation

On the second general line of policy measures to which our analysis has led, the creation of new assets vested in the poor, there is again no shortage of either central or state programmes. Among the major programmes in this category are the Drought Prone Areas Programme (DPAP), the Small Farmer Development Agency (SFDA), the Marginal Farmers and Agricultural Labourers (MFAL) programmes. Under these programmes, potentially viable farmers receive subsidised agricultural inputs, including credit, with the aim of encouraging particularly dairy farming, poultry, piggeries, sheep and goat rearing, fisheries and horticulture. Landless labourers receive employment through rural works programmes, and also a small homestead and assistance for construction of housing. In addition to these schemes sponsored by the central government a variety of schemes have been introduced at the state level.[18] Recently, the Reserve Bank of India, which has always played a significant role in strengthening the rural credit base, has announced the creation of a 'small farmers' window' for loans at concessional rates of interest to small farmers (Patel, 1977, p. 1223).

Many of these programmes have been given detailed evaluation by official and non-official agencies,[19] and a rather mixed picture emerges. Dairy farming and poultry have made significant progress, and, to a lesser extent, the tube-well programme. Land improvement, water management and multiple cropping programmes, on the other hand, have often lagged behind.[20] As seems to occur universally with programmes of this sort, some of the assistance, particularly credits, becomes diverted to the rich, while, on the other hand, some of the legitimate recipients are prevented, for institutional reasons, from benefiting. For instance, share croppers or tenants, particularly those with subdivided and fragmented holdings, cannot take advantage of credit facilities for the construction of minor irrigation works (Minhas,

1974, p. 114). In such cases effective land reforms become almost a precondition for the satisfactory operation of such schemes (Gadgil, 1970, p. 12).

While there is no doubt that such programmes are attempts in the right direction, as Sen stresses, 'the magnitude of this poverty, no matter which estimate one accepts, is so large that even if the schemes all prove highly successful no dramatic impact can be readily expected' (Sen, 1975, p. 144).

Outside agriculture, industrial policy in India also aims at both the creation of assets and the creation of employment in the small-scale sector for target groups. Direct assistance is given to small units through supply of raw materials, technical guidance and financial and marketing facilities. Certain industries are reserved exclusively for the small-scale sector and a cess is imposed on the large-scale sector to subsidise the small-scale industries (Kurien, 1978, pp. 455-61).

The past record of the sector is so far a mixed one. While the khadi and village industries, as well as small-scale industries, attained an annual rate of growth of 10 per cent between 1965 and 1978, hand-loom and powerloom have experienced only a small increase of 2.5 per cent per annum (Sandesara, 1978, p. 733). Difficulties in maintaining regular supplies of raw materials have proved a serious bottle-neck, while finance, servicing facilities and management abilities can all impose limitations (Gupta, 1978, esp. p. 13).

A general contention is that an increase in the income of the poor either through redistribution or through growth will automatically generate a demand for the products of such industries. Our own findings do not support this conclusion to any significant extent. As we have seen in Chapter 1, only around 10 per cent of the marginal increase in the consumption of the poor and the middle income groups both in the rural and urban areas is devoted to manufactures as a whole. Only a small part of this increase will be directed towards the small-scale industries. Therefore, if these industries are to become the corner-stone of policies for guaranteeing basic needs, the market for their products has to be found largely among consumers other than the poor. Moreover, on the export side the growing tendency to trade restrictions among the richer countries poses a major threat; according to the estimates of Cable and Weston (1978, p. 46) one job lost in the EEC in the production of fabric will create 15 to 20 jobs on the Indian subcontinent — and conversely for one job saved through protection against imports.

But in spite of these obstacles, further opportunities exist both for the creation of assets for the poor in small-scale industries and for employment creation, for both principal and subsidiary occupations. Fisheries, particularly freshwater fisheries, offer considerable potential. Fish are one of the richest sources of animal protein and of nitrogen for soil improvement. The technical knowledge required is not difficult even for illiterate people to acquire. And above all fish do not compete with crops for scarce land.[21]

The development of animal husbandry is a more debatable proposition, although it has been supported strongly by the National Commission on Agriculture (Government of India NCA, 1971). Animal husbandry provides a good source of income; on a small scale it can be easily managed by a poor family. However, it does require feedgrains and competes with humans for them. Although one of the richest sources of protein, animals are very expensive in terms of land. Since animal protein is not essential for human nutrition, at least at present grains claim priority.

The provision of rural water supplies, sanitation, housing and village roads also meets the objectives. They can provide substantial amounts of employment, generating incomes in local rural areas through this and the purchase of other necessary inputs, typically available within the villages.[22] By improving the environment, particularly in its public health aspects, they raise the productivity of labour. In addition, they, more than any other non-agricultural activity, can be phased in with seasonal agricultural activities and be accelerated in years of drought.

Land Reform

The relatively slow progress which is achieved in creating new assets for poor farmers under the schemes mentioned, combined with the highly skewed distribution of agricultural incomes, brings to the fore the issue of the structure of land ownership and makes the redistribution of land in favour of the poor a very tempting proposition.

Major land reforms, covering the abolition of intermediaries, the fixing of a ceiling on landholdings, the redistribution of land, and other legislation protecting tenancy, have always been, formally, important objectives of Indian planners and policy makers. But although legislation has been in force for virtually 30 years, the effective redistribution of land has been extremely limited.[23] Apart from the fact that most ceiling legislation contains a long list of exemptions (forests, fisheries, plantations, orchards) the ceilings for personal cultivation have been pitched high, often between 5 and 10 ha. of irrigated land, which, after allowance for evasions, yields only very limited amounts of surplus for redistribution.[24]

The question of the appropriate level for the land ceiling raises a major policy problem. Since the *per capita* availability of arable land to the rural population is around 0.4 ha., any ceiling significantly above 2 ha. per household would leave many rural households without land. Yet there is evidence (for example, Minhas, 1974, pp. 75-6) that many holdings of 2 ha. and below do not provide adequate levels of subsistence to the households which operate them. Thus, if the objective of land reform is to redistribute land in the form of holdings to individual households then many of these holdings will not be of viable size.[25] Moreover, the transfer to the poor of holdings below viable size is likely to prove self-defeating, in that the poor would in due course lose effective control of the land.[26] If, on the other hand, the object is to create or maintain economically viable farming units then many households must remain without land.

The problems associated with land availability and with the effective implementation of land reforms have led a number of authors to suggest that land redistribution policies, even radical ones, would not be sufficient to eradicate poverty.[27] The problems of viable size, in particular, have led to suggestions that some form of co-operative or collective operation of farming[28] may become inevitable, if radical redistribution policies are to be implemented. These continue to be highly controversial and sensitive issues in India. The conclusion seems inescapable, however, that if the aim is to guarantee the basic minimum to the poor, ceilings may have to be pitched at a much lower level than at present and serious thought given to the future organisational forms.

Concluding Remarks

This very brief review indicates that a variety of policies are currently operating which implement major elements of the strategies suggested by our analysis of the policy problem posed by the distribution of incomes and the position of the poor in India. These policies comprise consumption transfers, the transfer of assets and the creation of new assets and employment opportunities for the poor in a variety of sectors. Assessments of these policies, largely as offered by Indian commentators themselves, indicate a mixture of successes and frustration.

The essential finding of our analysis is that, given the present economic status of the poor, in terms of the pattern of income shares accruing to them, even substantial growth is unlikely to bring them significant benefit. Only positive policy action aimed at improving these income shares can substantially alter this. Our findings are relatively encouraging on the transfer 'costs', output requirements and income injections necessary to double the incomes of the poorest third of the population, which would represent a major contribution to providing basic needs for all. But given the low levels of incomes and assets over all in India the solution must come predominantly through growth, redirected towards ensuring a greater share for the poor.

When policies aimed at this objective are assessed, in conventional cost-benefit terms or otherwise, either before or after implementation, the nature of the alternative must also be kept in view. Unless effective policies are implemented, the economic prospects for the poor of India are likely to remain at least as bleak as at present, with all that this implies in human and political terms.

Notes

1. See Table 3.2, page 83.
2. See Table 4.3, page 99.
3. See Table 4.7, page 108.
4. See Table 1.5, page 38.
5. See Table 4.6, page 106.
6. See Tables 4.1, page 95, 6.2 and 6.3, pages 128, 130
7. See Table 4.2, page 97.
8. See Table 6.6, page 134.
9. See Table 4.8, page 111.
10. It is only in the latest Plan, for 1978-83, that the Planning Commission has used an 89-sector model with 11 agricultural sectors.
11. For a further discussion of personal savings in India see Lal (1977 and 1978).
12. The recent work of Adelman and Robinson (1978) is a major innovatory contribution in this direction.
13. For major reviews of some of these policies see Bardhan (1974, pp. 255-62), Dasgupta (1977), Sen (1975), Srinivasan (1974) and UN Department of Economic and Social Affairs (1975).
14. For a discussion and assessment of these programmes see Berg (1973, especially pp. 163-71).
15. Pingle (1978) further shows that changing the cropping pattern in favour of grains can bring an increase in employment.
16. Moreover, as Srinivasan (1974, p. 384) points out, where international prices are above domestic procurement prices, 'the domestic farmer is denied a price which the nation pays to the foreign farmer for imports'.
17. On the identification of the poor and people's participation in poverty programmes see Sinha (1976, p. 271) and Minhas (1974, p. 113).
18. See, for example, the Employment Guarantee Scheme of the State of Maharastra, discussed in Shahani (1977).
19. For a detailed evaluation of such programmes see Bardhan (1974a, pp. 255-62), Dasgupta (1977, pp. 296-313) and Sen (1975, Appendix B, pp. 135-45); see also Vakil (1977) and Gupta (1977).
20. For adoption of modern technology by farmers see Rao (1975), D'Sa (1977).

21. On fisheries and their employment potential see Jhingran (1978) and Swaminathan (1977).

22. See the analysis by Mathur (1978); also Sinha (1978).

23. See Srinivasan (1974, pp. 371-2), and Bardhan (1974, p. 256).

24. The weakness of land reform legislation in this respect does not invalidate its importance in altering the power structure in rural areas. As Myrdal points out, 'despite the weaknesses of the Indian legislation to abolish intermediaries, the reform should not be lightly dismissed. The former intermediaries may continue as ordinary landlords on a fairly large scale, but their reign as semi-feudal chiefs in rural districts has come to an end . . . A further effect of these reforms has been to alter the power structure in the rural areas. Generally, power in the villages is passing from the old absentee landlord class and its agents to an upper middle class composed of merchants, moneylenders, and peasant landlords often living in the villages' (Myrdal, 1968, p. 1310).

25. On the complex issue of viable farm sizes see particularly Raj Krishna (1962, 1964) and Venkatappiah (1969, 1970).

26. Redistribution of land raises another vital question relating to resource availability and economic and political power. For instance if 'due' compensation is paid, a 'fixed' capital asset is converted into a 'liquid' one, which in effect means that the 'dispossessed' land owners either use this for other agricultural activities (e.g. trade in grains, money lending) and thereby continue to wield economic power (see Reddy, 1978, p. 19) or recover their economic power by investing elsewhere. If the sum required for compensation is high, this may reduce the state's capacity to finance development expenditure in general or rural development in particular. For instance, if the provision of institutional credit is not increased significantly, then there is always the risk that the beneficiaries of a land redistribution will once again lose effective control of the land (Sinha, 1976, pp. 50-1).

27. See Srinivasan (1974, p. 372).

28. The Government of India and the Planning Commission at one time thought in terms of co-operative village management (Government of India Planning Commission, 1964, pp. 194-5) and the Nagpore Resolution of the All-India Congress Committee (1959) went as far as to suggest a compulsory pooling of land, though with the farmers retaining their proprietary rights (Kothari, 1959, pp. 1032-3; see also Khusro, 1969, 1973). Subsequently, the idea of compulsion was abandoned.

APPENDICES

1. Sector Classification

1. Rice
2. Wheat
3. Pulses and gram
4. Other foodgrains
5. Fruits, nuts, vegetables and spices
6. Cotton
7. Jute
8. Oilseeds
9. Sugarcane
10. Tobacco
11. Other agriculture (including fodder and by-products)
12. Animal husbandry (including milk, meat, fish and eggs)
13. Plantations
14. Tea and coffee
15. Forestry products
16. Coal
17. Miscellaneous coal and petroleum products
18. Iron ore
19. Crude oil
20. Other minerals
21. Sugar
22. Gur
23. Vanaspati
24. Vegetable oils
25. Cigarettes and cigars
26. Other tobacco products
27. Other food products
28. Cotton textiles
29. Cotton yarn
30. Jute textiles
31. Woollen yarn and fabrics
32. Manmade fibres
33. Art silk fabrics
34. Silk and silk products
35. Other textiles
36. Wood products (including furniture)
37. Paper and paper products
38. Leather footwear
39. Leather
40. Other leather products
41. Rubber products
42. Fertiliser
43. Chemicals
44. Plastics
45. Cosmetics and medicines
46. Petroleum products
47. Cement
48. Refractories
49. Iron and steel
50. Non-ferrous metals
51. Metal products (including domestic utensils and containers)
52. Non-electrical machinery
53. Electrical household goods
54. Radios
55. Other electrical goods
56. Bicycles
57. Motor bicycles
58. Motor vehicles
59. Aircraft and ships
60. Railway equipment
61. Other transport equipment
62. Watches and clocks

63. Miscellaneous scientific equipment
64. Other industries
65. Printing and publishing
66. Electricity
67. Rural housing construction
68. Urban housing construction
69. Other construction
70. General pucca construction
71. Railway transport
72. Other transport
73. Education
74. Entertainment
75. Medical care
76. Domestic service
77. Other services (including trade and
        storage, and public administration
        and defence)

2. Sector Grouping used for Summary Tables *

Groups	Sector numbers
a. Agriculture	1-11
b. Animal husbandry	12
c. Total agriculture (a+b)	
d. Mining, forestry and plantations	13, 15, 16, 18, 19, 20
e. Total primary (c+d)	
f. Food, drink and tobacco	14, 21, 22, 23, 24, 25, 26, 27
g. Textiles and leather footwear	28, 29, 30, 31, 34, 35, 38
h. Wood, glass, ceramics and cement	36, 47, 48
i. Leather and leather products (except footwear)	39, 40
j. Chemicals, fertiliser and petroleum products	42, 43, 46
k. Basic metals, metal products and other engineering	49, 50, 51, 52, 53, 55, 56, 57, 58, 59, 60, 61
l. Other manufacturing	17, 32, 33, 37, 41, 44, 45, 54, 62, 63, 64, 65
m. Total manufacturing (f-l)	

n. Total services (including electricity,
       construction and transport)   66-77

---

* In some tables minor variants of this grouping have been adopted.

Adelman, I. and Morris, C.T. (1973) *Economic Growth and Social Equity in Developing Countries* (Stanford University Press, Stanford)

——. and Robinson, S. (1978) *Income Distribution Policy in Developing Countries: A Case Study of Korea* (Oxford University Press for World Bank, London)

Ahluwalia, M.S. (1978) 'Rural Poverty and Agricultural Performance in India', *The Journal of Development Studies*, vol. 14, April

—— and Chenery, H.B. (1974) 'A Model of Distribution and Growth' in Chenery, Ahluwalia *et al.* (1974)

Ahmad, K. (1978) 'Towards Equality: Consequences of Protective Discrimination', *The Economic and Political Weekly*, 14 January

Ahmed, M. and Bhattacharya, N. (1972) 'Size Distribution of per Capita Personal Income in India', *The Economic and Political Weekly* (Special Number reprinted in Srinivasan and Bardhan (eds) (1974))

Austin, G. (1966) *The Indian Constitution: Cornerstone of A Nation* (Clarendon Press, Oxford)

Ballentine, J.G. and Soligo, R. (1978) 'Consumption and Earnings Patterns and Income Distribution', *Economic Development and Cultural Change*, vol. 26, July

Bardhan, P.K. (1974) 'The Pattern of Income Distribution in India: A Review' in Srinivasan and Bardhan (eds) (1974)

—— (1974a). 'India' in Chenery, Ahluwalia *et al.* (1974)

—— and Rudra, A. (1978) 'Interlinkage of Land, Labour and Credit Relations: An Analysis of Village Survey Data in East India', *The Economic and Political Weekly* (Annual Number), February

Baster, N. (1970) *Distribution of Income and Economic Growth* (United Nations Research Institute for Social Development, Geneva)

Berg, A. (1973) *The Nutrition Factor: Its Role in National Development* (Brookings Institution, Washington DC)

Bhagwati, J. (1973) 'Education, Class Structure and Income Equality', *World Development*, vol. 1, May

Bhatty, I.Z. (1974) 'Inequality and Poverty in Rural India' in Srinivasan and Bardhan (eds) (1974)

Blitzer, C.R., Clark, P. and Taylor, L. (eds) (1975) *Economy-Wide Models and Development Planning* (Oxford University Press for World Bank, London)

Bronfenbrenner, M. (1971) *Income Distribution Theory* (Aldine, Atherton, Chicago and New York)

Brown, A. and Deaton, A. (1972) 'Models of consumer behaviour', *Economic Journal*, vol. 82, December

Cable, V. and Weston, Ann (1978) *ODI Study of EEC Access Barriers Facing South Asian Exports and South Asian/EEC Commercial Cooperation* (mimeo.) (ODI, London)

Casley, D.J., Simaika, J.B. and Sinha, R.P. (1974) 'Instability of Production and its Impact on Stock Requirement', *Monthly Bulletin of Agricultural Economics and Statistics*, vol. 23, May

Chakravarty, S.K. Datta, U. and Srinivasan, V. (1960) 'Share of Urban and Rural Sectors in the Domestic Product in India in 1952-53' in Rao, V.K.R.V., Sen, S.R., Divatia, M.V. and Datta, U. (eds) (1960), *Papers on National Income and Allied Topics*, vol. 1, Indian Conference on Research in National Income (Asia Publishing House, New Delhi)

Chatterjee, G.S. and Bhattacharya, N. (1974) 'On Disparities in Per Capita Household Consumption in India' in Srinivasan and Bardhan (eds) (1974)

—— (1974) 'Between State Variations in Consumer Prices and Per Capita Household Consumption in Rural India' in Srinivasan and Bardhan (eds) (1974)

Chenery, H.B. (ed.) (1971) *Studies in Development Planning* (Harvard University Press, Cambridge, Mass.)

—— Ahluwalia, M.S., Bell, C.L.G., Duloy, J.H. and Jolly, R. (eds) (1974) *Redistribution with Growth* (Oxford University Press for World Bank and Institute of Development Studies, University of Sussex, London)

—— and Duloy, J.H. (1974). 'Available Planning Models' in Chenery, H.B., Ahluwalia, M.S., Bell, C.L.G., Duloy, J.H. and Jolly, R. (eds) (1974)

—— and Raduchel, W.J. (1971) 'Substitution in Planning Models', in Chenery, H.B. (ed.) (1971)

—— and Watanabe, T. (1958) 'International Comparisons of the Structure of Production', *Econometrica*, vol. 26.

Chinn, D. (1977) 'Distributional Equality and Economic Growth: The Case of Taiwan', *Economic Development and Cultural Change*, vol. 26, October

Chitnis, S. (1972) 'Education for Equality: Case of the Scheduled Castes', *The Economic and Political Weekly* (Special Number)

Clark, P.B. (1975) 'Intersectoral Consistency and Macroeconomic

Planning' in Blitzer, C.R., Clark, P.E. and Taylor, L. (eds) (1975)

Cline, W.R. (1972) *Potential Effects of Income Redistribution on Economic Growth* (Praeger, New York)

—— (1975) 'Distribution and Development: A Survey of Literature', *Journal of Development Economics*, vol. 1

CSO (*see* Government of India)

Dandekar, V.M. and Rath, N. (1971) *Poverty in India* (Indian School of Political Economy, Poona)

—— (1971a) 'Poverty in India' Parts I and II, *The Economic and Political Weekly*, 2 and 9 January

Dasgupta, B. (1977) *Agrarian Change and the New Technology in India* (United Nations Research Institute for Social Development, Geneva)

D'Sa, M. (1977) 'Technological Change in Agriculture: The Development Experience of Tamil Nadu', unpublished Ph.D. thesis, Glasgow University

Duskin, L. (1972) 'Scheduled Caste Politics' in Mahar, J.M. (ed.), *The Untouchables in Contemporary India* (The University of Arizona Press, Tucson)

Farbman, M. (1974) 'A Methodology for estimating statewise size distributions of income in rural India' (mimeo.) (ILO, World Employment Programme Working Paper, Geneva)

Figueroa, A. (1975) 'Income Distribution, Demand Structure and Employment: The Case of Peru' in Stewart, F. (ed.), *Employment, Income Distribution and Development* (Frank Cass, London), pp. 20-31; reprinted from *Journal of Development Studies*, vol. 11, January

Floud, J. (1975) 'Education and Equality: A Perspective from the West', *Journal of Higher Education*, vol. 1, Autumn

Foxley, A. (1976) 'Redistribution of Consumption: Effects on Production and Employment in Foxley, A. (ed.), *Income Distribution in Latin America* (Cambridge University Press, Cambridge); *Journal of Development Studies*, vol. 12, April (1976)

Gadgil, D.R. (1970) 'Inaugural Speech at the Workshop on Small Farmers and Agricultural Labour held in New Delhi on the 17th and 18th July', reproduced in Planning Commission (1970), *Workshop on Small Farmers and Agricultural Labour* (Government of India, New Delhi)

Gaiha, R. (1977) 'A Model of Manpower Planning for India', unpublished Ph.D. thesis, University of Manchester

—— (1978a) 'A Comparative Analysis of Occupational Profiles in

Private and Public Sectors in India', in Sinha *et al.* (1978), Part II
—— Vashishtha, P. and Mohammad, S. (1978) 'A Comparative Analysis of Educational Profiles of Workers in Private and Public Sector Manufacturing Industries in India – A Cross-Section Analysis' in Sinha *et al.* (1978), Part II

Ganguli, B.N. and Gupta, D.B. (1976) *Levels of Living in India* (S. Chand, New Delhi)

Ghosh, A. (1968) *Planning, Programming and Input-Output Models: Selected Papers on Indian Planning* (Cambridge University Press, Cambridge)

Gopalan, C. and Narasingarao, B.S. (1971) *Dietary Allowances for Indians* (Indian Council of Medical Research Special Report no. 60, Delhi)

Goreux, L.M. (1960) 'Income and Food Consumption', *Monthly Bulletin of Agricultural Economics and Statistics*, vol. 9, October

Government of India, Central Statistical Organisation (1964) *Report on the Middle Class Family Living Survey 1958-59* (Department of Statistics, Cabinet Secretariat, New Delhi)
—— (1967) *Brochure on Revised Series of National Product for 1960-61 and 1964-65* (Department of Statistics, Cabinet Secretariat, New Delhi)
——, (1969) *Estimation of Savings in India 1960-61 to 1965-66* (Department of Statistics, Cabinet Secretariat, Government of India, New Delhi)
—— (1975) *National Accounts Statistics 1960-61 to 1972-73: Disaggregated Tables* (Department of Statistics, Ministry of Planning, New Delhi)
—— (1976) *National Accounts Statistics 1960-61 to 1974-75* (Department of Statistics, Ministry of Planning, New Delhi)
—— Ministry of Information (1975) *India: A Reference Annual 1975* (New Delhi)
—— Ministry of Labour, Employment and Rehabilitation (1968) *Family Living Survey Among Industrial Workers 1958-59: General Report* (New Delhi) (this survey was conducted in 50 centres and individual reports are available for each centre)
—— (1969) *Report of the National Commission on Labour* (New Delhi)
—— (1973) *Report of the Committee on Unemployment* (New Delhi)
—— National Commission on Agriculture (1971) *Interim Report of the National Commission on Agriculture on Milk Production Through Small and Marginal Farmers and Agricultural Labourers* (Ministry of Agriculture, Government of India, New Delhi)

——, National Sample Survey (1971) *Tables with Notes on Household Consumer Expenditure and Enterprise for Rural and Urban Areas of India; Integrated Household Survey (Schedule 17)*, Nineteenth Round: July 1964-June 1965, no. 189 (Department of Economic Affairs, Ministry of Finance, New Delhi)

— (1972) *Tables with Notes on Villages and Towns in India: Some Results*, Twenty-second Round: July 1967-June 1968, no. 196 (Department of Economic Affairs, Ministry of Finance, New Delhi)

— (1975) *Some Results on Small Scale Manufacture in Rural and Urban Areas*, Twenty-third Round: July 1968-June 1969, no. 205 (Department of Statistics, Ministry of Planning, New Delhi)

— (1976) *Tables with Notes on Small-scale Manufacture in Rural and Urban Areas*, Twenty-third Round: July 1968-June 1969 (Department of Statistics, Ministry of Planning, New Delhi)

— Planning Commission (1954) *Agriculture and Community Development* (New Delhi)

— (1956) *The Second Five Year Plan* (New Delhi)

— (1964) *Report of the Committee on Distribution of Income and Levels of Living, Part I: Distribution of Income and Wealth and Concentration of Economic Power* (New Delhi)

— (1969) *Report of the Committee on Distribution of Income and Levels of Living, Part II: Changes in Levels of Living* (New Delhi)

— (1970) *Report of the Committee of Experts on Unemployment Estimates* (New Delhi)

— (1973) *A Technical Note on the Approach to the Fifth Plan of India, 1974-79* (New Delhi)

— (1973a) *Draft Fifth Five Year Plan 1974-79, Parts I & II* (New Delhi)

— (1978) *Draft Five Year Plan 1978-83* (New Delhi)

Griffin, K. (1971) *Green Revolution - An Economic Analysis* (United Nations Research Institute for Social Development, Geneva)

— (1975) *The Political Economy of Agrarian Change* (Macmillan, London)

Gupta, B.N. (1977) 'Rural Employment; Past Failures and New Strategy', *The Eastern Economist*, 5 August.

Gupta, D.B. (1973) *Consumption Patterns in India: A Study of Inter-regional Variations* (Tata McGraw-Hill Publishing, Bombay)

—— (1978) 'Employment Implications of Cottage Industries' in Sinha *et al.* (1978), Part II

Hazari, B. and Krishnamurthy, J. (1970) 'Employment Implications of India's Industrialization: Analysis in an Input-Output Framework',

Review of Economics and Statistics, vol. 52

Hirschman, A.O. (1958) *The Strategy of Economic Development* (Yale University Press, New Haven)

Ho, Y-M (1976) 'Income Redistribution and its Effects on Factor Demand in Taiwan: A Simulation Approach', *Southern Economic Journal*, October

Hopkins, M. (1977) *Basic Needs Approach to Development Planning - A View* (mimeo.) (ILO, World Employment Programme Research Working Paper, Geneva)

Inayatullah (1972) *Cooperatives and Development in Asia: A Study of Cooperatives in Fourteen Rural Communities of Iran, Pakistan and Ceylon* (United Nations Research Institute for Social Development, Geneva)

Indian Council of Medical Research (ICMR) (1967) *Report of Nutrition Work Done in States in 1967* (this Report is published annually) (Hyderabad)

International Labour Office (1970) *Towards Full Employment: A Programme for Colombia* (International Labour Office, Geneva)

—— (1971a) *Matching Employment Opportunities and Expectations: A Programme of Action for Ceylon; Technical Papers* (International Labour Office, Geneva)

—— (1971) *Matching Employment Opportunities and Expectations: A Programme of Action for Ceylon: Report* (International Labour Office, Geneva)

—— (1976) *Employment, Growth and Basic Needs* (International Labour Office, Geneva)

—— (1977) *The Basic Needs Approach to Development* (International Labour Office, Geneva)

Iyengar, N.S. (1960a) 'On Methods of Compiling Engel Elasticities from Concentration Curves', *Econometrica*, vol. 28

—— (1960b) 'On Problems of Estimating Increase in Consumer Demand', *Sankhya*, vol. 22

—— and Jain, L.R. (1973) *On a Method of Estimating Income Distribution* (Indian Statistical Institute Planning Unit Discussion Paper no. 97, December)

—— and —— (1974) 'Changing Patterns of Consumption in India', *Artha Vijnana*, vol. 16, September

Jeffrey, R. (1978) 'Allopathic Medicine in India: A Case of Deprofessionalisation?', *The Economic and Political Weekly*, 21 January

Jhingran, V.G. (1978) 'Employment Potential of Freshwater Fisheries in India' in Sinha *et al.* (1978), Part II

Johnson, B.F. (1970) 'Criteria for the Design of Agricultural Development Strategies', *Food Research Institute Studies*, vol. 11

Johnson, G.E. and Whitelaw, W.E. (1974) 'Urban-Rural Income Transfers in Kenya: An Estimated-Remittances Function', *Economic
Development and Cultural Change*, vol. 22

Kadekodi, G.K. (1978) 'The Cost of a 'Balanced' Diet' in Sinha *et al.*
(1978), Part II

—— and Pearson, P.J.G. (1978) 'Estimation of Consumption Elasticities in India' in Sinha *et al.* (1978), Part II

Kansal, S.M. (1965) 'Preliminary Estimates of Total Consumption
Expenditure in India 1950-51 to 1963-64' (mimeo.) (Indian Statistical Institute Discussion Paper no. 5, 16 September)

Khusro, A.M. (1969) *The Economics of Land Reform and Farm Size in
India* (Institute of Economic Growth, Delhi)

—— (1973) *The Economics of Land Reform and Farm Size in India*
(Macmillan, New Delhi)

Kothari, R.F. (1959) 'From Service to Farming Co-operatives', *The
Economic Weekly*, July

Krishna, Raj (1962) 'The Optimum Firm and the Optimum Farm', *The
Economic and Political Weekly*, 6 and 13 October

—— (1964) 'Some Production Functions for the Punjab', *Indian Journal of Agricultural Economics*, July-December

Kurien, C.T. (1978) 'Small Sector in New Industrial Policy', *The
Economic and Political Weekly*, 4 March

Lal, D. (1976) 'Agricultural Growth, Real Wages, and Rural Poor in
India', *The Economic and Political Weekly*, 26 June

Lal, R.N. (1977) *Capital Formation and Its Financing in India* (Allied
Publishing Co., Bombay)

—— (1978) 'Estimation of Capital Formation by Main Industrial
Categories' in Sinha *et al.* (1978), Part II

Lipton, M. (1977) *Why Poor People Stay Poor: A Study of Urban Bias
in World Development* (Temple Smith, London)

Lisk, F. (1977) 'Conventional Development Strategies and Basic Needs
Fulfilment', *International Labour Review*, March-April

—— and Werneke, D. (1976) *Alternative Development Strategies and
Basic Needs* (mimeo.) (ILO, World Employment Programme Research
Working Paper, Geneva)

Madan, G.R. (1966) *Economic Thinking in India* (S. Chand & Co.,
Delhi)

Majmudar, M. (1977) *Regional Income Disparities, Regional Income
Change and Federal Policy in India, 1950-51 to 1967-68: An Empiri-*

cal Evaluation (mimeo.) (Department of Economics, University of Dundee, Dundee)

Manne, A.S. (1974) 'Multi-sector models for development planning', *Journal of Development Economics*, vol. 1

Mathur, G.C. (1978) 'Employment Potential of Housing Construction Under Different Technologies' in Sinha *et al.* (1978), Part II

Mathur, P.N. *et al.* (1968) 'Input-Output Table 1963' in Mathur, P.N. and Venkatramaiah, P. (eds), *Economic Analysis in Input-Output Framework* (P.N. Mathur, Poona)

Minhas, B.S. (1970) 'Rural Poverty, Land Redistribution and Development Strategy', *Indian Economic Review*, vol. 5, April

—— (1974) *Planning and the Poor* (S. Chand & Co., New Delhi)

Morawetz, D. (1974) 'Employment Implications of Industrialisation in Developing Countries: a Survey', *Economic Journal*, vol. 84, September

Morley, S.A. and Smith, G.W. (1973) 'The Effect of Changes in the Distribution of Income on Labor, Foreign Investment and Growth in Brazil' in Stepan, A. (ed.), *Authoritarian Brazil: Origins, Policies and Future* (Yale University Press, New Haven)

—— and Williamson, I.G. (1974) 'Demand, Distribution and Employment: The Case of Brazil', *Economic Development and Cultural Change*, vol. 23

Mukherjee, M. (1969) *National Income of India: Trends and Structure* (Statistical Publishing House, Calcutta)

—— (1972) 'National Income Statistics' in Rao, C.R. (ed.), *Data Base of Indian Economy* (Indian Statistical Society, Calcutta, and Indian Econometric Society, Hyderabad)

Myrdal, G. (1968) *Asian Drama: An Inquiry Into The Poverty of Nations*, 3 vols. (Allen Lane, The Penguin Press, Harmondsworth)

National Council of Applied Economic Research (1962) *Urban Income and Savings* (National Council of Applied Economic Research, New Delhi)

—— (1964-5) *All India Rural Household Survey*, vol. 1 (1964), vol. II (1965) (National Council of Applied Economic Research, New Delhi)

—— (1965) *All India Rural Household Survey, II, Income, Investment and Savings* (National Council of Applied Economic Research, New Delhi)

—— (1966) *All India Consumer Expenditure Survey, Vol. I, Methodology* (National Council of Applied Economic Research, New Delhi)

—— (1967) *All India Consumer Expenditure Survey, Vol. II, Pattern of Income and Expenditure* (National Council of Applied Economic

Research, New Delhi)

—— (1972) *All India Household Survey of Income, Saving and Consumer Expenditure* (National Council of Applied Economic Research, New Delhi)

—— (1975) *Changes in Rural Income in India 1968-69, 1969-70, 1970-71* (National Council of Applied Economic Research, New Delhi)

National Institute of Nutrition (1971) *Diet Atlas of India* (Hyderabad)

NCA *see* Government of India

NSS *see* Government of India

Ojha, P.D. and Bhatt, V.V. (1974) 'Pattern of Income Distribution in India: 1953-55 to 1963-65' in Srinivasan and Bardhan (eds) (1974)

Panikkar, K.M. (1963) *The Foundations of New India* (George Allen & Unwin, London)

Patel, I.G. (1977) 'Bank Credit Must Reach The Poorer Strata of Priority Sector', *The Eastern Economist*, 23 December

Patwardhan, S. (1973) *Change Among India's Harijans* (Orient-Longman, New Delhi)

Paukert, F. and Skolka, J. (1972) 'Redistribution of Income, Patterns of Consumption and Employment: A Framework of Analysis' (mimeo.) (International Labour Office, Geneva)

—— and Maton, J. (1976) 'Redistribution of Income, Patterns of Consumption, and Employment: A Case-Study for the Philippines' in Polenske, K.R. and Skolka, J.V. (eds), *Advances in Input-Output Analysis* (Ballinger, Cambridge, Mass.)

Pearson, P.J.G. and Pingle, G. (1978) 'Determination of Shares in Value Added from Crop Production in Agriculture' in Sinha *et al.* (1978), Part II

Pillai, S.K. (1975) 'Estimation of Livestock Numbers and Products' in Dandekar, V.M. and Venkatramaiah, P. (eds), *Data Base of Indian Economy: Role of Sample Surveys* (Indian Statistical Society, Calcutta, and Indian Econometric Society, Hyderabad)

Pingle, G. (1978) 'Potentialities for Increased Employment Through Changes in Crop Pattern' in Sinha *et al.* (1978), Part II

Polenske, K.R. and Skolka, J.V. (eds) (1976) *Advances in Input-Output Analysis* (Ballinger, Cambridge, Mass.)

Pyatt, G. and Thorbecke, E. (1976) *Planning Techniques for a Better Future* (International Labour Office, Geneva)

——, Roe, A.R. and Associates (1977) *Social Accounting for Development Planning; with Special Reference to Sri Lanka* (Cambridge University Press, Cambridge)

Raj, K.N. (1959) 'Resources for the Third Plan: An Approach', *The Economic and Political Weekly* (Annual Number)

Ramanujam, M.S. and Raghavan, K. (1978) 'Estimation of Sector-wise Employment for the Indian Economy: 1967-68' in Sinha *et al.* (1978), Part II

Ranadive, K.R. (1968) 'Pattern of Income Distribution in India, 1953-54 to 1959-60', *Bulletin of Oxford University Institute of Economics and Statistics*, August

Rao, C.H.H. (1975) *Technological Change and the Distribution of Gains in Indian Agriculture* (Macmillan, New Delhi)

—— (1977) 'Agricultural Growth and Rural Poverty: Some Lessons From Past Experience', *The Economic and Political Weekly* (special issue), August

Rao, V.K.R.V. (1965) 'Economic Growth and Rural Urban Income Distribution 1950-51 to 1960-61', *The Economic and Political Weekly*, February

—— (1974) *Growth with Justice in Asian Agriculture: An Exercise in Policy Formulation* (United Nations Research Institute for Social Development, Geneva)

Rasmussen, P.N. (1956) *Studies in Intersectoral Relations* (North Holland, Amsterdam)

Reddy, P.J. (1978) 'Indian Constitution and Social Justice' in Sinha *et al.* (1978), Part II

Rodgers, G.B., Hopkins, M. and Wéry, R. (1978) *Population, Employment and Inequality: BACHUE-Philippines* (Saxon House, Farnborough)

Roy, B. (1975) 'A Study of the Survey Data used in India to Estimate Savings, Capital Formation and Allied Aggregates' in Dandekar, V.M. and P. Venkatramaiah (eds), *Data Base of Indian Economy*, vol. II (Statistical Publishing Society, Calcutta)

Roy, J. and Dhar, S.K. (1960) 'A Study on the Pattern of Consumer Expenditure in Rural and Urban India' in *Studies on Consumer Behaviour* (Asia Publishing House, Bombay)

Rudra, A. (1972) 'Savings, Investment and Consumption' in Rao, C.R. (ed.) *Data Base of Indian Economy*, vol. I (Statistical Publishing Society, Calcutta)

Saha, R.P. (1975) 'Cost of Cultivation Surveys' in Dandekar and Venkatramaiah (eds) (1975)

Sahota, G.S. (1978) 'Theories of Personal Income Distribution: A Survey' in *Journal of Economic Literature*, vol. XI, March

Saluja, M.R. (1968) 'Structure of Indian Economy: Inter-Industry

Flows and Pattern of Final Demands 1964-65', *Sankhya*, Series B, vol. 30

—— (1972) 'Structure of Indian Economy, 1964-65, Input-Output Relations Among 144 Sectors', *Sankhya*, Series B, vol. 34

—— (1978) 'A Brief Note on the Construction of GDO Input Output Table for 1967-68' in Sinha *et al.* (1978), Part II

Sandesara, J.C. (1978) 'Small Industry Production in 1982-83: A Quick Comment', *The Economic and Political Weekly*, 29 April

Schermerhorn, R.A. (1978) *Ethnic Plurality in India* (University of Arizona Press, Tucson)

Schultz, S. (1976) 'Intersectoral Comparison as an Approach to the Identification of Key Sectors' in Polenske, K.R. and Skolka, J.V. (eds), *Advances in Input-Output Analysis* (Ballinger, Cambridge, Mass.)

Sen, A.K. (1975) *Employment, Technology and Development* (Clarendon Press, Oxford)

Shahani, R.T. (1977) 'The Employment Guarantee Scheme of Maharastra', *The Eastern Economist*, 25 November.

Sharma, I.R.K. (1974) 'Inequalities in Personal Income Distribution in India', *Margin*, vol. 6, April

Sher, G. (1975) 'Justifying Reverse Discrimination in Employment', *Philosophy and Public Affairs*, vol. 4, no. 2

Singh, N.K. (1977) 'Oppression of Scheduled Castes', *The Economic and Political Weekly* 22 October

Sinha, A. (1977) 'Pauperisation of the Adivasis', *The Economic and Political Weekly*, 22 October

Sinha, J.N. (1978) 'Rural Employment Planning: Dimensions and Constraints', *The Economic and Political Weekly* (Annual Number), February

Sinha, R.P. (1961) *Food in India* (Oxford University Press, Bombay)

—— (1966) 'An Analysis of Food Expenditure in India', *Journal of Farm Economics*, vol. 48, February

—— (1976) *Food and Poverty: The Political Economy of Confrontation* (Croom Helm, London)

—— and Hay, F.G. (1972) 'Analysis of Food Expenditure Patterns of Industrial Workers and Their Families in a Developing Country', *The Journal of Development Studies*, vol. 8

—— Pearson, P.J.G., Kadekodi, G. and Gregory, M. (1978) *Poverty, Income Distribution and Employment: A Case Study of India* (mimeo.) (Glasgow, Delhi, Oxford Project Report, Glasgow)

Sinha, S.N. (1978) 'Employment Potential of Road and Bridge Construction Under Different Technologies' in Sinha *et al.* (1978), Part II

Soligo, R. (1973) 'Factor Intensity of Consumption Patterns, Income Distribution and Employment Growth in Pakistan' (mimeo.) (Program of Development Studies, Rice University, Paper no. 44)

Srinivas, M.N. (1962) *Caste in Modern India and Other Essays* (Asia Publishing House, London)

Srinivasan, T.N. (1974) 'Income Distribution: A Survey of Policy Aspects' in Srinivasan and Bardhan (eds) (1974)

—— and Bardhan P.K. (eds) (1974) *Poverty and Income Distribution in India* (Statistical Publishing Society, Calcutta)

Stern, J.J. (1977) 'The Employment Impact of Industrial Investment A Preliminary Report' (World Bank Staff Working Paper no. 255, World Bank, Washington, DC)

Stewart, F. (ed.) (1975) *Employment, Income Distribution and Development* (Frank Cass, London)

—— (1978) 'Too dear to Work', *Mazingira*, vol. 5

Streeten, P. and Burki, S.J. (1977) *Basic Needs: An Issue Paper* (mimeo.) (World Bank, Washington DC)

Subramaniam, V. (1971) *Social Background of India's Administrators* (Publications Division, Ministry of Information and Broadcasting, Government of India, New Delhi)

Sulkhatme, P.V. (1977) 'Malnutrition and Poverty', Ninth Lal Bahadur Shastri Memorial Lecture, 29 January (ICAR, New Delhi)

—— (1977a) 'Incidence of Undernutrition', *Indian Journal of Agricultural Economics*, vol. XXXII, no. 3, July-September

Sunman, T.M. (1973) 'Short-run Effects of Income Distribution on Some Macro-Economic Variables: The Case of Turkey' (mimeo.) (Program of Development Studies, Rice University, Paper no. 46)

Swaminathan, M.S. (1977) 'Indian Agriculture at the Crossroads', Presidential Address delivered at the 37th Annual Conference of the Indian Society of Agricultural Economics, New Delhi. 12-27 December, published in *Indian Journal of Agricultural Economics*, vol. XXXII, no. 4

Taylor, L. (1975) 'Theoretical Foundations and Technical Implications' in Blitzer, C.R., Clark, P.B. and Taylor, L. (eds) (1975)

Tokman, V.E. (1974) 'Distribution of Income, Technology and Employment: An Analysis of the Industrial Sectors of Ecuador, Peru and Venezuela', *World Development*, vol. 2

—— (1975) 'Income Distribution, Technology and Employment in Developing Countries: An Application to Ecuador', *Journal of*

Development Economics, vol. 2
—— (1976) 'Income Distribution, Technology and Employment in the Venezuelan Industrial Sector' in Foxley, A. (ed.), *Income Distribution in Latin America* (Cambridge University Press)
United Nations Department of Economic and Social Affairs (1975) *Poverty, Unemployment and Development Policy: A Case Study of Selected Issues with Reference to Kerala* (New York)
United Nations Economic Commission for Asia and Far East (1970) *Sectoral Output and Employment Projections for the Second Development Decade* (Bangkok)
—— (1972) *Intraregional Trade Projections, Effective Protection and Income Distribution*, vol. III (Income Distribution, Development Programming Techniques series, no. 9, Bangkok)
United Nations Food and Agricultural Organisation and World Health Organisation (FAO/WHO) (1973) *Energy and Protein Requirements: Report of a Joint FAO/WHO Ad Hoc Expert Committee* (Geneva)
United Nations Food and Agricultural Organisation (1975) *Population, Food Supply and Agricultural Development* (Rome)
—— (1977) *The Fourth World Food Survey* (Rome)
United Nations Research Institute for Social Development (1966) *The Level of Living Index* (mimeo.) (Geneva)
—— (1970) *Contents and Measurement of Socio-economic Development* (mimeo.) (Geneva)
US Agency for International Development (USAID) (1975) *The Tamil Nadu Nutrition Study* (mimeo.) (Haverford)
Vaidyanathan, A. (1974) 'Some Aspects of Inequalities in Living Standards in Rural India' in Srinivasan and Bardhan (eds), (1974)
Vakil, C.N. (1977) 'Growth with Stability', *The Eastern Economist*, 21 October
Venkatappiah, B. (1969) *Presidential Address* to Indian Society of Agricultural Economics (Waltair)
—— (1970) 'Small Farmers' Problems and Programmes' (National Food Congress, India)
Venkatramaiah, P., Kulkarni, A.R. and Argade, L. (1972) 'Input-Output Table for India, 1963' in *Artha Vijnana*, vol. XV
Weisskoff, R. (1973) 'A Multi-Sector Simulation Model of Employment, Growth and Income Distribution in Puerto Rico: A Re-Evaluation of "Successful" Development Strategy' (mimeo.) (Economic Growth Center, Yale University)
—— (1976) 'Income Distribution and Export Promotion in Puerto

Rico', in Polenske, K.R. and Skolka, J.V. (eds), *Advances in Input-Output Analysis* (Ballinger, Cambridge, Mass.)

—— and Wolff, E. (1977) 'Linkages and Leakages: Industrial Tracking in an Enclave Economy', *Economic Development and Cultural Change*, vol. 25

Zarambka, P. (1972) *Toward a Theory of Economic Development* (Holden-Day, San Francisco)

—— (1974) 'Transformation of Variables in Econometrics' in Zarembka, P. (ed.), *Frontiers of Econometrics* (Academic Press. New York and London)

INDEX

170

For Product Safety Concerns and Information please contact our EU
representative GPSR@taylorandfrancis.com Taylor & Francis Verlag GmbH,
Kaufingerstraße 24, 80331 München, Germany

Printed and bound by CPI Group (UK) Ltd, Croydon, CR0 4YY
08/05/2025
01864370-0018